WELCOME
To The Family

WELCOME
To The Family

Edited by
Steve Lawhead

Designed by
Nathan Young

ZONDERVAN PUBLISHING HOUSE
OF THE ZONDERVAN CORPORATION
GRAND RAPIDS. MICHIGAN 49506

Campus Life Publications, Inc.
Carol Stream, Illinois 60187

WELCOME TO THE FAMILY
Copyright © 1982 by Youth for Christ International

First printing March 1982

Library of Congress Cataloging in Publication Data

Main entry under title:
    Wecome to the family.

    1. Christian life—1960-   —Addresses,
essays, lectures.   I. Lawhead, Steve.
BV4501.2.W4174   248.4   81-23173
ISBN 0-310-35491-9   AACR2

Printed in the United States of America

Photos in this book are used for illustration; they do not necessarily represent the actual people.

Contents

WELCOME
To The Family

Imagine this: It is 1854 and you are five years old. You are living in the streets of New York City. Homeless, alone. No one wants you; no one cares for you. You are an orphan.

Your world is a stinking slum — people jammed together in misery. Your clothes are rags, barely enough to keep out the cold and wet. Your only friends are others just like yourself. They teach you to steal bread from unattended windows, to peddle paper flowers, to snatch ladies' purses on the street and wallets from men who visit the bordellos.

Your life is meager survival from day to day. You wander the filthy streets as an urban nomad.

Then one day, beyond your wildest imaginings, a man comes to you and tells you there is a way out, a way to a new life far from the slums and streets. You go with him to a place where you are given warm clothes and food. Then you climb aboard a train which chugs its way into America's heartland. Days pass and unfamiliar landscapes — forests and fields — slide by the windows. What is happening? Where are you going?

When the train stops at last, you get off and are whisked into the waiting arms of a kind and gentle man who takes you to your new home. He adopts you; gives you a new name, his name. He makes you a part of his family, showering you with all the things you never had before — love, acceptance, security.

This scenario is not fiction. It is literally true — nearly 100,000 children endured this cruel nightmare and awoke to a fairytale-happy ending. The "Orphan Train," as it came to be called, made it possible.

In the last half of the nineteenth century, hundreds of thousands of immigrants poured into New York City. Families broke apart when many parents never reached America alive, leaving armies of young orphans to roam the city streets alone. Then a young minister named Charles Brace, appalled at the desperate plight of these youngsters, hit upon a daring strategy.

Along with a small band of concerned adults, Brace began writing letters and sending flyers to small Midwestern towns which lined the railroad tracks in a straight line west across the

country. Stops were arranged, the train was advertised, and children were rounded up on the train with no specific destination in mind but with the blind hope that some compassionate person at some point along the route would adopt a child.

The Orphan Train was the last hope of salvation. And for nearly 100,000 young people, that hope became a miraculous reality.

Today the story of the Orphan Train is a sentimental and inspiring part of American history. But think about it. It is more: a parable with a far deeper meaning. Every Christian shares something of the story of the Orphan Train.

Every one of us — every person on earth — comes into this world a spiritual orphan. We are lost, homeless, alone. Yet, some of us find the way to safety: Jesus. Through him we become the sons of God — an image the Bible uses over and over again. When we become Christians we are adopted into God's own family. And like the orphans on the Orphan Train, revolutionary changes begin taking place in our lives.

Becoming a Christian involves more than joining a club, or subscribing to an idealistic lifestyle. Much more. Jesus said it was as radical and jolting as being "born again." The early Christians said that people who joined their ranks became "new creatures." So much happens all at once that it often takes years to learn its full extent, and what it means.

In many ways becoming a Christian is like being adopted. Suddenly we have a new father, a new home, a new family, a new identity. Any one of those changes can overwhelm a person, but taken all together they are mind-boggling. Sadly, many new Christians never fully understand what has happened to them until much later in life. That's too bad, because the more fully we grasp the significance of what it means to be a Christian, the more immediate will be our enjoyment of our incredible good fortune.

We present this book to help you celebrate what it means to join this new family. You may not think of Christianity as something to be enjoyed in the same way you would enjoy a birthday cake or a summer vacation. But being a Christian *is* enjoyable, perhaps the way growing up in a loving family, or growing close to a wonderful friend is enjoyable. Learning about God and growing close to him is the very source of joy.

We at CAMPUS LIFE have had a lot of experience welcoming new members into the family. We know the jolts, the growing pains, and rough places. We hope this book can ease the transition and help you to begin enjoying this very special time.

Welcome to the family!

Steve Lawhead

Just Like A Father

My father can beat your father!" Probably every little kid has said that. We all want to believe that our fathers can do anything — bigger, better, faster than anyone else's father. And for a time it seems to be true. But as we grow older we begin to see the faults; little inconsistencies, weaknesses, and human frailties surface that we never noticed before. One day our father disappoints us and we realize he isn't perfect. He doesn't wear a red cape and a suit with an "S" on the front — he's only human like everyone else. Sometimes that comes as a shock. Maybe we resolve in our childish heart never to trust anyone again. We'd only be disappointed.

But as Christians we have a father who is perfect in every way: God. Like the spiritual orphans we are, we're adopted by God and become his children. Suddenly we have an advantage we never dared to dream of: we are heirs of the King of the universe. We have a father who not only loves us, but also has the power to change our lives and circumstances for the better. He wants us to be happy, and, more, he wants us to learn to live in a way that will bring his love to others. Toward this end he gives each of his children special gifts that enable them to carry out the special assignments he has for them to do. God has plans for his children, and like any father he expects them to live in a way that will do credit to the family name.

But, there are problems here: How do we get to know an invisible father? And how do we find out what plans he has for us? Those are tough assignments. However, we can start by learning who God is and how he works. The following chapters will discuss these important areas and help develop a clearer picture of the only perfect father.

The Waiting Father

Gabriel Heatter, the famous newscaster in the days of radio, used to begin his newscast every evening by saying, "There's good news tonight!" And all over the country people would stop and listen because no matter how bad things were — a depression, a war, a national disaster — Heatter would/find something good to report, and everyone would feel a little better.

Jesus came to bring good news, too. Only his is the ultimate good news. "Listen," he says, "you can go home again!"

There's a joke making the rounds that goes something like this: "I've got good news and bad news for you. The good news is that Jesus is coming back real soon." What's the bad news? "He's really mad!"

Who wouldn't be mad? Look around. Look at the shape the world is in: war, hunger, disease everywhere. In the cities crime breeds unchecked; greed runs rampant through business, industry and welfare systems; the courts choke on injustice, the highest elected officials of government stuff their pockets with both hands; families break up so fast the splits can't be counted; pollution of the earth's resources continues full tilt, every decent human emotion is debased by the popular media; the technologically advanced nations teeter on the edge of nuclear oblivion. . . . The whole world is in one big, hopeless mess.

God left the world in our care; he gave it to us to watch over, to nurture, to cultivate. We blew it. God has every right to be angry. He has every right to blast us all into smoking smithereens, and then scatter the ashes across a billion galaxies. He could do it, too.

But he won't.

He holds back for the same reason that he refrains from dropping the murderer in his tracks at the scene of the crime or from striking the liar speechless in mid-sentence or from withering the pickpocket's hand in mid-pick. But why? Why doesn't he exact punishment on the spot?

Jesus explained it this way. He said that God's goodness, his grace, was such that he "makes his sun rise on the evil and on the good, and sends the rain on the just and on the unjust." In other words, God is content

by STEVE LAWHEAD

Tim Stafford

to hand out the same treatment to everyone whether or not they deserve it. Think about it — if we all got exactly what we deserved this planet would look like one big ghost town. The human race would have been exterminated long ago.

For now, however, God's goodness restrains him from making judgment. You might say he's giving everyone the benefit of the doubt until all the votes are in. We all live in a state of grace — God's grace. He's treating us not as we deserve, but as his own children whom he loves and wants to have with him.

The Fair Deal

Some people, Christians included, have a problem with that. How can God let all the evil people run free? It doesn't seem fair. So long as they don't get caught, the cheaters, rapists, and muggers get whatever they go after. And the mean-mouthed, the ugly-minded, the utterly selfish come out even better because there are no laws against their crimes. Meanwhile, those who love, who sacrifice to feed the hungry, who care about the people unable to care about themselves — old people, battered children, mentally handicapped, those too low on hope to ever pull themselves up — those who risk all they have on loving others get nothing. And when you pray for your grouchy neighbor, struggle to be kind, spend your own money to help someone you don't even know, you get nothing.

That's not fair!

But God is fair. He *is* keeping track. Punishment will come to those who deserve punishment. And he will ultimately reward those who have rewards coming. But if that's the case, why keep everyone in suspense? Why not ring down the final curtain, dispense the rewards and call it quits? What is God waiting for? Why doesn't he just get it over with?

There is no simple answer to that one. But we get flashes of God's motives from time to time throughout the Bible. Jesus put it all

How can God let all the evil ones run free? It doesn't seem quite fair.

together when he told a story so poignant and powerful that after 2,000 years it still excites those who read it. And no one who reads it can help but glimpse something of God's care and concern for his children.

The Wayward Boy

The story is found in Luke 15 and, boiled down, it goes like this:

A man had two sons. The youngest son demanded his share of the inheritance, promptly sold it off for ready cash and took the money and went to another country to live it up. He wasted all his money on loose living and wild parties and woke up one day to find it was gone. He'd squandered it all. About this time a severe famine hit and he began to starve. He took the only job he could find — as servant to a hog farmer — and went to work. The boy became so hungry that even the dry husks he was feeding the pigs looked good to him. But no one would give him anything.

Finally he came to his senses and said to himself, "At home even my Dad's hired men have food enough and more besides. And here I am dying of hunger! I'll go home and tell my father, 'I have sinned against heaven and you. I am no longer fit to be called your

Bob Combs

son. Please take me on as a hired hand.' "

So he started for home and when he was still a long way off his father saw him coming, and was filled with love and pity and ran to his son and hugged him.

The boy started to object, saying, "Father,

I am no longer worthy — " But his father cut him off saying to the servants, "Quick! Bring the finest clothes in the house and dress him. And a jeweled ring for his finger; and the best shoes for his feet. And kill the calf we've been saving for a celebration! We must have a party, for this son of mine was dead and has come back. He was lost and is found again." So the party began.

This story is known as the Parable of the Lost Son. But that title conceals something of the meaning because it focuses on the wrong person in the story, the son. The ultimate theme of the story is not the wayward son, but the waiting father. In fact, that's the title given to this parable by some who have guessed its deeper significance — The Waiting Father. For, it is not only a story of a boy gone bad and his recovery; it is also about the father who loved the boy so much he stood out on the road looking for him to come home again.

We aren't told many details; none of Jesus' stories are very long. They are painted in simple, masterly strokes and move quickly. It is for us to fill in the details.

What about the father then? We are told he gave his son his inheritance without question, well before the proper time, out of love for him. He wanted his son to have the good things his wealth could buy. The boy squandered it, however, and couldn't handle his freedom very well. But when he decided at last to come back home again, did the wayward boy have to crawl before the gates, weeping and begging to be taken back? Did his father say, "Yes, you can come back, but you must earn your keep and work to pay back every penny I gave you"?

The boy never reached the gates because his father ran to meet him. How did the father know the boy was coming? Jesus tells us that while the son was still a long distance off the father saw him. The father couldn't have known the boy was returning unless he had been standing out on the road waiting for him to come back, scanning the horizon

What an unexpected turn of events — not a scolding, but a party.

and hoping to catch a glimpse of his son coming home. We aren't told this, but it seems likely that the father had stood there waiting, week in and week out, blindly hoping that someday his son would return.

And when the boy finally appeared, there were no angry words, not even a well-deserved reprimand (the boy fully expected one). In fact, the young man didn't even get half-way through his repentance speech — the father brushed it aside and called instead for a feast, a celebration! What an unexpected turn of events. Not a scolding, but a party. Not punishment, but forgiveness. Welcome home! All is forgiven!

Good News

This is really the good news Jesus came to bring us: God's incredible forgiveness. There is a home waiting for everyone who wants it. And you don't have to beat down the doors, either. Just turn back to God — you'll be met before you can even reach the gate. The father is waiting.

Perhaps this is also the reason why such joy and festivity ring out from this story. You can't help but notice it whenever you read it. Wherever forgiveness like this is proclaimed, there is cause for celebration. If we could actually hear this story for the first time, if we could only read it as it was really meant to be, it would shock us. Good news! News so good we can't imagine it, because what Jesus is telling us is that everything about God is completely different from anything we feared. God is not against us, he is for us. His hands hold not punishment, but healing love and acceptance. He forgives fully, completely, and wholeheartedly.

No one is excluded from his forgiveness, and there is no limit to it. As Christians we make mistakes, we sin. But God is patient; he doesn't explode in righteous judgment. When we stumble he's more concerned that we get back on our feet and on the right path. So he forgives and encourages, he loves and accepts without qualification, without hesitation. This astonishing forgiveness is available to everyone.

Perhaps that is why this world continues day by day — God is not willing that anyone should be lost. He continually waits for his wayward children to come back. He even sent Jesus to bridge the distance between heaven and earth, so that there would be no mistake that he really wanted everyone to come home again. Now, that may not be what some people think of as fairness; it's far too lenient, too soft. But that, Jesus says, is the good news. There is a homecoming for all of us who want it because there is a home and there is a father waiting to begin the celebration.

Get Tough Jury

John Hafner is speaking to his high school contemporary affairs class. Glancing nervously around the room, he begins to relate the story of a crime in the neighborhood.

The crime involves two kids breaking into a home. They threaten a family with a gun, tie them up, rob them and depart. The kids need no money; they are out for sport. The frightened victims mean nothing to them. John graphically fills in the details, and the class is quiet, struck with what a foolish, dangerous thing the two kids have done. Most of them had read about the crime in local papers. Now, two years later they still remember the shocking effect it had on the family.

After telling the story, John gives the students a chance to respond:

"We need the death penalty for people like that."

"Too bad they didn't resist arrest so the cops could have shot them. That's all they deserve."

"Life in prison is too good for guys like that."

"But," John interrupts, "these were young men with a long life ahead of them. Shouldn't they be helped to change, to grasp new values, to rehabilitate themselves? Isn't society better served if they can become good citizens instead of just being stored in a lock-up?"

The class isn't buying. They've heard of too many cases soft on criminals. Get tough, take revenge, throw the book at them.

Finally one student asks John, the moderator, "What would *you* do with them?"

"I'll answer that, but first you should know I'm prejudiced. The crime we are discussing is not fiction. *I am one of the two guys who committed it.*"

The class is startled. John Hafner is a senior, a good student, neat, highly respected, their class president.

He continues. "Two years ago, when I was 15, I did rob and terrorize that family. I am here today because the things you suggested were *not* done. The police used restraint. Even though they knew we were wrong and had been armed, I wasn't put in some hole of a prison to grow bitter. I was sent to a juvenile ranch where I got good counseling from people who care, and I got involved in sports, school, and work.

"It was there I met the Lord and became a Christian. God gave me a strong base on which to rebuild my life and change my values. After eleven months, I was released and came to this school.

"I'm glad someone — in this case a judge and a probation officer — cared enough to give me a chance to rebuild my self-respect, pay my debt to society, and contribute something useful to this world. And God gave me a chance for a new life. He erased my record. None of you would have given me that chance.

"Did I deserve a break? No, but I'm glad I got it."

The class is silent for a long pause, until the bell signals the end of the period. Sobered, the students get up and walk quietly into the busy hallway.

Nineteen hundred years ago an apostle named Paul said something similar: "But isn't this unfair for God to let criminals go free and say that they are innocent? No, for he does it on the basis of their trust in Jesus who took away their sins. Then what can we boast about doing, to earn our salvation? Nothing at all. Why? Because our acquittal is not based on our good deeds; it is based on what Christ has done and our faith in him.

"So it is that we are saved by faith in Christ and not by the good things we do."

—Romans 3:26–28
The Living Bible

by Gordon McLean

Who Is God?

What do Hare Krishnas, Moonies, Moslems, and Hindus have in common? They all say they know who God is. The only trouble is none of their answers agree. Christians, too, say they know who God is. What is more, they say they know him personally.

Asking the question "Who is God?" is a little like asking "What is life?" or "How many angels can dance on the head of a pin?" — every person you talk to will give you a different answer. Too many different answers add up to no answer at all.

Christians say they know who God is; they say they know him personally. And after two thousand years they have learned some of his many characteristics and have discerned certain traits in his personality. The Bible details many of God's attributes that men have consistently found to be present.

These characteristics paint a broad picture of God and tell us a little of what he is like. If you're going to spend your life in God's family, you should know something about him.

He Is Ever-Present

Our finite minds cannot conceive of what it means to have no boundaries, no limits, no restrictions of any kind. We are like children growing up in a small concrete cell with only a two-dimensional sketch of the outside world — to us everything is flat and contained. But God is infinite; he knows no restraints. He can be everywhere, all the time.

We often think of God as Superman — merely a bigger, better or more streamlined version of ourselves. We take up so many square inches as we stand in our stocking feet, filling out our skins with so much muscle and bone. God cannot be measured in this way; his boundaries would stretch from one galaxy to another if he had any limits at all. Our minds shrink from trying to picture such vast dimensions.

God is forever and always. That may sound like a valentine sentiment, but in God's case it is literally true. He stands outside of time, which means that he does not age like we do. He has no beginning and no end, neither birth nor death. From where he stands he can see the future and past as easily

as the present. And since he sees the whole parade of human history at a glance, he can be found constantly working through time to bring about his plans. But isn't God limited by time like we are? Not at all. Time is an element we are immersed in, like fish immersed in water. God reaches down into our element, like a fisherman reaching down into water to accomplish his goals. No place or time extends beyond his grasp.

He Is a Person

What we have just described does not sound like anyone we may be able to get close to. Perhaps the most difficult attribute to accept is that God is a person, that he has a personality — our own personalities, in fact, are probably individual reflections of his. God has a mind; he communicates to others. He possesses emotions — feelings that involve him in caring deeply about people. And unlike some sort of cosmic robot or electronic brain, he invites us to know him as intimately as he knows us. He is not, as some say, an impersonal force, a vague power that has no conscience or organization. God can be approached on a personal basis, one person to another, because he wants us to understand him, to love him, to experience him as a friend and father.

He Is an Artist

All artists show something of themselves in their work, and God is no exception. This earth and everything in it are his works of art.

Many people have the idea that God is cold, distant, and lifeless, yet his handiwork bursts with the throbbing warmth of life and creativity. He didn't make just two or three kinds of plants or animals — he made thousands! From bears to hummingbirds, elephants to insects, mice to milk cows. There are 400,000 different species of beetles alone! Then there are plants of every description, from the giant redwoods to tiny, invisible plankton. Every nook and crevice of this planet throbs with life at every level of existence.

As an artist, God works on a vast canvas, calling his creation into existence out of nothing by a single word. Everything God touches leaps to life; his creation reflects his joy in living things.

He Is the Boss

Since God created everything, he knows how it's supposed to work. So, he provided an instructional manual, the Bible, to show how he intended his creation to run.

He left man in charge of looking after his handiwork — the earth, wildlife, our fellow human beings — like the boss who leaves the foreman in charge of running the shop. And we are responsible to him for how we've done our share of the work. God sets the standard and judges the results. He left strict rules for us to follow, and stiff penalties for breaking those rules.

But God is not a judge without compassion. He knows our limitations and weaknesses, and leaps to our defense when we fail to live up to his standards. He longs to cover our mistakes with his all-forgiving grace. This doesn't make him a spineless marshmallow of a boss. Not at all. Forgiving us isn't a weakness. He is simply more concerned with making the right kind of people than with punishing offenders. And we can trust his judgment because he never makes mistakes or allows prejudice to cloud his vision. His word is perfect justice — never weak, never confused by contradicting evidence, never distorted, never selfish or grudging.

He Is Mysterious

What we know of God is only what he had chosen to reveal to us. He remains beyond our examination; he can't be trapped, tagged, or

Rod Gerig

tested. His ways defy discovery.

Throughout history he has shown various facets of his multifaceted nature to people at various times. Yet, there is so much more of him than can be understood at one time. Man has always had a rather imperfect picture of God.

In a supreme effort to remedy this problem God came to earth himself. The fullest expression of his character came 2,000 years ago in the form of a man: Jesus. In Jesus we see God in flesh and blood — real, touch-

able, approachable. Jesus is God in human clothing, walking and talking with those around him, and demonstrating once-and-for-all-time what God is really like.

He Is Love

What Jesus demonstrated beyond all doubt was God's overwhelming love for his creation. It is a love that has no equivalent in human terms — a love that can raise the dead, make blind men see and crippled men walk. Jesus gave the world a taste of God's love it has never forgotten.

The Bible sums up this all-encompassing love by stating simply, in the briefest description of God you will find anywhere, "God is love" (1 John 4:16). This says more than that he is loving, or that he has an unusual amount of love to go around. What the Bible is trying to tell us is that God is love itself. Do not, however, make the mistake of assuming the reverse, that love is God. The feeling you have for a cocker spaniel puppy, or your Aunt Minnie, or your boyfriend or girlfriend is not God. Perhaps the best way to think about this is that love is God's nature, his character, his personality. His "skin" and "stuffings" are love; everything he thinks and all that he does is love.

This in no way limits God, or reduces him to a fluttery emotion. The kind of love we hold for each other, the warm feeling we get, the super emotional charge that leaps through us when we are near someone very dear to us — they're all the merest shadow of the love that God is. They are the ripple that laps at our feet, the bracing spray of an entire ocean of love. We usually only dabble at the edges of love. Maybe this is best. If we could totally grasp all that love is we would fall speechless because we would see God himself.

Wounded Lover

When we broke up, I felt fiercely angry at Judy.

I didn't want to be so angry; I'd been taught that anger wasn't good. At any rate, could I really blame her for dumping me? Who was to say I didn't deserve it?

I could reason my way around it, but I couldn't put it out of my mind. Again and again I created imaginary scenes where I lashed out at her, exploding in righteous fury. In my imagination, she would look at me with moist eyes and admit that she was wrong. She would ask me to forgive her and help her improve. She would cry.

I knew those fantasies were ridiculous; I told myself so. But I couldn't stop the anger. It kept coming back, often without warning or prompting. It followed me wherever I went.

It wasn't that I didn't like her; I did. In fact, the intensity of my feelings showed me how appallingly much I *did* like her. I could have shook her, yelled at her, kissed her into submission — *anything* to get her back. Anything to snap her to her senses.

Those powerful emotions are gone now, and I haven't even seen Judy in a long time. But I still remember how violently angry I felt. I am basically an easygoing person. Nothing else in my life has ever made me feel so powerfully angry as her rejection.

Recently I've discovered an anger as violent and powerful as my own: God's. The Bible mentions God's anger in more than 300 places, such as "That day will be a day of wrath, a day of terrible distress and anguish, a day of trouble and ruin, of darkness and gloom, a day of clouds and blackness . . . " (Zeph. 1:15, NIV).

That *bothers* me. The thought that God gets angry is disturbing. So what do I do? Edit the Bi-ble? Do I cut out the part of the New Testament where Jesus takes a whip to people in the temple? I've wanted to many times. An angry God isn't very pleasant for me to think about. Especially a God who almost seems to relish venting his anger at his own helpless people.

Some have pointed out that God has a right to punish. People break the rules he has established for their own good. If he is just, if he sticks to his word, he has to punish.

But somehow that doesn't solve my problem. Yes, God has the right to punish. But doesn't that make him rather impossible to love? His punishment sounds cold and legalistic, like a sentence meted out by a stern, black-robed, totally objective judge. I can respect him, but love him?

But there is another possibility, one that is related to my anger at Judy. What if God's fiercest anger comes for the same reason mine does — not when "rules" are disobeyed, but when love is rejected?

What makes me the angriest? Someone breaking my rules? No: wounded love. Could it be the same with God?

I read the Book of Hosea with that in mind. Hosea tells the story of a man who marries a whore. She keeps rejecting his love and going off with other men. Again and again the husband goes after her and brings her back. The story, Hosea says, is a picture of what we do to God. We are married to him, but keep going off with other loves, rejecting his.

Could it be that God is so angry because he loves so much? Yes, I think so. (You're never upset over something you care nothing about.) So of course he is angry! The angriest person is always the wounded lover. God loves people — loves

by TIM STAFFORD

them passionately. *That* is why he is so angry when he is rejected. Then is his anger like mine: vain, ridiculous and impotent? Is it vengeful, meant to destroy people? Of course not. But his anger does share one thing with the kind of anger I felt. The point of my anger was to bring Judy back to me. I didn't want to destroy her. I wanted her to respond. I wanted to yell, sulk, shake her — *anything* — to get her to pay attention to me. Anger was the one thing she couldn't ignore. She could ignore carefully thought-out statements, flowers, invitations — but not anger.

I've begun to believe that's the point of God's anger. His anger screams, "I love you! I want you to act right, to respond lovingly to my love. I can't stand what you're doing to me!"

I believe that's his attitude toward me, today.

When my love grows cold toward him, when I get preoccupied with other things and leave him out, when I don't put enough into my relationship with him to keep it from becoming a bore, my life deteriorates. Sometimes things get visibly messed up; other times only an invisible emptiness grows inside.

In either case it isn't an accident. There are no "accidents" for Christians. It is God, the Wounded Lover, crying to me, "Stop it! I can't stand what you're doing." And under this cry I begin to see what I've been doing, and I'm forced to respond to his love.

That is the way the real God is. He is a God of fire, of anger. Above all, he is a God of love — passionate, absorbing, demanding love. He loves us — and his anger proves it.

Looking For A Face

God, of course, is more than just a list of qualities on paper. To really understand him you have to move from knowing about God to knowing God. You have to meet him face to face. Is that possible? Tim Stafford, a Campus Life editor, asked the same question and found an answer that will surprise you.

Have you ever noticed how important faces are? You spend hours peering at your own in the mirror. You collect wallet-sized photos of other people. No one gives away wallet-sized pictures of an ankle or hand. It's the face that counts.

Look at a face objectively and its attraction seems strange. It's a bulbous stretch of skin with all kinds of knobs and holes. There are two shiny, slick balls that never stay still. Discolored skin around a loose, spongy slit periodically pulls back to reveal two rows of sharp, porcelain knives. Above the two rapidly-shifting bright-colored balls, two crescents sprout hair from a smooth, oily surface. On the whole, you wouldn't call it an attractive collection.

Yet we do find it attractive. What's more, we have the idea that the face tells us something important about its bearer. I'm not referring to whether it smiles or frowns, but to something more basic. Something of a person's character, we think, is built into the face.

That's why it's hard to fall in love through letters or over the phone (and why a lot of people who do are very disappointed when they finally meet). You never feel you *know* someone until you've seen his or her face. And even when you have seen it, you need to see it again and again. Relationships carried on by letter tend to fade.

This is exactly the problem men have had with God over the centuries. Everything is carried on over the phone. We never *see* him.

Not that there hasn't been any contact. The Old Testament records thousands of years of God's messages to his people. Many in those times saw him in visions — visions powerful enough to throw them cringing to the ground. Moses, a man so close to God he talked to him "as a man speaks to his friend," asked to actually see God and was allowed to see part of him (but not his face). There were plenty of miracles, plenty of direct messages

by TIM STAFFORD

— but *never once* did God show his face. The New Testament looks back on it and summarizes the frustration by saying "no one has ever seen God" (John 1:18).

Was God teasing them? Did he send them notes and messengers, giving them clues on what he was like and how they could find him, only to deliberately disappear around the corner, leaving the tantalizing echo of his laughter? Some must have wondered.

Fireworks in Reverse

Then something enormous happened — something that split history in two. God came personally to earth as a man, an event so extraordinary people have been trying to describe it ever since. One classic description of God's entry into our world is "fireworks in reverse."

Think of the grand finale at a big Fourth of July celebration: the sky erupting in dazzling irridescence — shocking golds, reds, greens; electrifying blues and silver lighting up the night. The air is shattered by the roar and thunder of explosive salutes. Yet a moment before, all that radiance and power was simply packaged in a plain brown wrapper.

When Jesus came to earth, his grandeur stretched beyond space and time. He had created everything — stars, planets, molecules, atoms — and all creatures great and small moved and rejoiced in him. A library of books does not begin to trace the scope of what he was and is.

He laid aside his glory, however, becoming a helpless baby born to an insignificant peasant couple in an obscure village in a backward corner of the world. The might and authority that rules all heaven and earth was focused in Mary's womb.

When he was born he entered the world he himself had made. He was man, yet still somehow he was God. He restrained all his vast unlimited power for our sakes, and took on a man's limitations.

God put himself on public display for thirty years. He walked our roads, talked our language, wore our clothes. He had a face. About him John wrote, "Christ was alive when the world began, yet I myself have seen him with my own eyes and listened to him speak. I have touched him with my hands" (1 John 1:1, Living Bible).

Paul called him "the image of the invisible God." In Jesus, God smashed for all time the complaint that he didn't care about people — that he was too haughty to come out of the clouds and let people confront him. God was more than willing. He pulled no tricks to protect himself. He jostled elbow to elbow with crowds of the sick and the poor. There were no "Do Not Touch" signs on him. Anyone could look him in the eye.

But here is a strange thing: he wasn't recognized. Even the men who lived with him, Jews who had studied the results of thousands of years of God-finding lessons, didn't realize who he was until it was nearly too late. It wasn't that he wore a disguise. He deliberately fulfilled all the predictions and statements that had been made about God. His personality was God's personality. But he had left his majestic glory behind. (Perhaps that was necessary. His was the same glory and majesty that, even in a vision, had shattered grown men.)

There was another problem: men's shortsightedness kept them from seeing the total Jesus. They saw a bit of his kindness here, a bit of his sternness there, but they couldn't put it together. They took his boldness to be bragging. They thought his forgiveness was too soft. The more they saw of his real character, the less they liked it. In fact, when he flatly told them who he was, they spat in his face. God had finally removed the veil and shown himself, and they spat — then killed him.

A few didn't reject him, though. After the resurrection they realized whose face they had been looking into for those years. Their joy in the discovery shocked the world. But soon after they realized who he was, Jesus left again, promising to come back.

Once more people were left in darkness. God had hidden his face again.

But had he? He left his followers behind, and he sent his Spirit to fill them. They were to be his body on earth — the face of Christ to a world that has never seen him.

We carry on that job. No matter how ugly an individual part appears — the fleshy nose, the slick eyes — the whole body of Christians presents a fact that should be unmistakably Christ's. Our love should represent his. Our morals should mirror his. If the world has a hard time recognizing him, could it be because we don't act quite the way he told us to? In our faces, can others see the Lord's?

Getting Personal

Most people would say it is impossible to become intimate friends with someone who hasn't been seen in nearly 2,000 years. Yet that's precisely what Christians say they do; they even encourage others to do the same. What exactly do they mean?

When I first became a Christian I heard a phrase that confused me a little. Sometimes I would be with some of my Christian friends and one of them would ask, "How's your relationship with the Lord?" Or, I would overhear a group of Christians talking and someone would say, "That book really helped my personal relationship with God."

I wasn't sure what they meant when they said they had a personal relationship with God. God is invisible, so how do you have a "personal relationship" with him? You can pray to him, worship him, read in the Bible about him — but is that the same as having a personal relationship with him?

I was confused so I kept quiet whenever anyone spoke of a personal relationship with God, because, as a new Christian, I wasn't exactly certain I had a personal relationship. I felt a little guilty, too, even though I wasn't sure what they meant.

It sounded as though they had some sort of hotline to heaven, some sort of inside deal that I didn't know about yet. I kept wondering, "When will I get my personal relationship with God?" I didn't dare ask anyone about this; he or she might think I wasn't a Christian at all. Maybe this was something reserved only for "real" Christians. I began to doubt whether I really was a Christian.

Then something happened that seemed to confirm my pessimistic diagnosis. I decided to quit my job because it was eating into my homework and after-school hours too much. I wanted to go out for tennis and there was no way I could manage both. My Christian boss was absolutely confident I was doing the wrong thing. He sat me down and told me that God didn't want me to quit. "I was down on my knees talking to God for three solid hours last night," he said. "And God definitely spoke to me. He told me you weren't supposed to quit this job."

I countered by telling him I hadn't received any messages like that from God.

by TIM STAFFORD

Bob Taylor

"But were you praying for three solid hours? Has God told you that you're *supposed* to quit?"

I had to say no. I hadn't heard any voices at all. Did God talk to all Christians like that? If so, why didn't he talk to me?

So, I concluded that if a personal relationship was made up of direct communication and warm, peaceful feelings, I couldn't claim to have a very good one.

Inside me, a lot of guilt began to grow. What was I doing wrong? Wasn't I a "real"

Jim Whitmer

Growing Guilt

Another thing I noticed was that the people who said they had a personal relationship with God often described it as something like a warm, peaceful feeling. A beautiful hymn about prayer expresses this: "And he walks with me, and he talks with me, and he tells me I am his own; And the joy we share as we tarry there none other has ever known."

That, for me, was foreign to my experience. I could almost sense what they were talking about; I had maybe felt like that once or twice. But not all the time, not every day.

Christian? But no matter how much I cried out to God — and I can remember some particularly agonizing times when I asked God for just one word of reassurance — I didn't get that personal relationship I looked for. God wasn't as close as my brother. He wasn't even as close as my grandfather. Only once in a while, when I wasn't looking for it, did God surprise me and seem to come very close.

I didn't become more comfortable with the phrase overnight. It took a long time for me to realize that there was something very personal about my relationship with God —

something that had always been there.

What I think we should mean when we say we have a personal relationship with God is this: God is a person, not an institution, an idea or ideal, not a principle or the unity of everything. He is a person; all of his nature was expressed in Jesus Christ, a person who walked, talked, ate dinner and had friends.

And I am a person, too: not a dream, not a machine, not an animal, not a body only or a spirit only.

Now how do persons relate? Not necessarily as buddies. They may write letters, or talk over the phone. Age differences may keep their relationship rather formal. But certain things do happen.

1. *Persons communicate ideas.* Your point of view is gradually, subtly affected by the other. So God communicates ideas, helping me to understand his way of thinking.

2. *Persons affect each other through love and encouragement.* You can love your car to death, but you won't make it run any better. Persons, by loving each other, do help each other "run better." God affects us tremendously, gradually, by the amazing way he loves us.

3. *When a person loves you, you frequently begin to model your life after that person.* My parents have loved me longer and harder than anyone else, and it's amazing how, more and more, I find their traits in me. When my friends love me, I find myself starting to talk like them and go to the same places they like.

So my relationship with God is personal in that I model myself after him. I begin to want to be like Jesus.

4. *When people give advice to friends, they do it politely.* They don't force the other

to respond, even if they are quite sure they are right.

That is true of God. He never forces himself or his ideas on me. He is gentle, and a gentleman who respects my freedom.

5. *Finally, persons help each other deal with trouble.* And God helps me just that way.

When I say I have a personal relationship with God, I mean this: God is a person, and I treat him that way. I am a person, and God treats me that way.

It does not mean that we communicate in a conversation: Moses did, apparently, but I don't. I talk, believing that God is listening; so far he has not talked back, though sometimes he has used my feelings and thoughts to point me in a different direction than I was ready to go. He has done most of his talking in the Bible.

I have to admit, I would like it better if I could see God and have a genuine conversation with him. I wish I didn't have to muster up faith to believe that he is constantly with me; I would like that to be obvious. But evidently that doesn't matter as much as I think. What matters is that I learn to believe God even when it's not obvious that he cares. What matters is that I allow him, as an unspeakably loving and completely wise person, to affect me, a person who needs that love and wisdom. He is doing that, and that is why I am no longer nervous about the phrase "personal relationship."

Make no mistake: I am not content. I would like to have a conversation with God. I would like to be with him "physically," whatever that would mean. I would like to have his love absolutely, unshakably obvious.

Someday, I believe, I will.

Am I Talking To Myself?

What if you could drop a quarter in the nearest pay phone and get God on the line? How many times a week would you call him? How many times a day?

We need that daily contact with God — that's how our relationship deepens; it's how we grow. And praying is even easier than talking on the phone — you don't need a quarter to pray, and you can do it anytime, anywhere. What could be easier than just talking to God? Yet for many new Christians, praying is anything but easy. Problems arise that can nag and fritter away your concentration and desire to pray, problems that can make praying a dull, tedious chore. We asked noted writer and speaker Charlie Shedd to tackle some of the most common prayer problems posed by anxious Christians. Here's what he had to say.

Your mind wanders. You have a list of things you want to talk to God about, but instead you find yourself worrying about the test you've got at school that day. Before you know it your time's gone, and you've used it to daydream. You're frustrated. How can you ever pray if your mind wanders like that?

The wandering mind is a challenge to our discipline. There are two or three things that my wife Martha and I do with it. One is, we *let* our mind wander, and we pray for the thing that we wander to. Let me give you an example. Suppose you start praying about a trip you're looking forward to, and then your mind might wander and think, "Hey, I've got to pick up my ticket." So then you pray, "Thank you, Lord, for plane tickets. God, how we live! Here I am sitting in an airplane 33,000 feet in the air and I have this little ticket. Bless the people who make out those tickets and help me to keep it in my hands so that I don't lose it. Bless the people who have lost tickets. I saw that sexy girl in the airport the other day running up to the counter; she'd left her ticket there. Was she sexy! She had a dress on that just drove me nuts. Lord, bless this girl and thank you for beautiful women and thank you that I am a sexual creature." This kind of prayer is really fun.

by CHARLIE SHEDD

Rick Smolan

33

No Answer

When your mother was dying, you prayed with all your heart and soul she would be healed. You believed she would be. But instead she died. You can't see why. You grope for a reason. Did you lack faith? Or was it that God doesn't really care or have time for you?

This is getting right down to the meat of the coconut because we all have things we want that we can't have. We would like to design things that aren't in God's design.

The secret has to be, I think, that our friend, our great, wonderful, loving God, this inner Christ, has answers we don't know anything about. This is where faith comes in. We have to believe that he means it when he says, "Our lives are eternal. What you see happening here is just the reverse side of the rug. It isn't as beautiful on this side as it is on the finished side. You have to believe me that under all the circumstances, I know what's best." Years from now you will probably say, "Hey, I see it all now!"

And I would even go further and say, "This friend is not able to do some things." If you think your friend can do everything, you're wrong. Yes, there are areas where God limits himself. Like the little boy says, "Can God make two hills without a hollow?" There has to be a valley between two hills or there aren't two hills. So there are some laws God made that he does not break.

Now there's the additional question of whether you had enough faith to make the healing happen. Personally, I don't think you make things happen when you pray. I think you get in the condition where you can let God work.

Faith is not so much pep-talking yourself, or grinding up your ambition or abilities so that things will happen, as it is getting yourself in shape to let things happen the way God wants them. If you were in that position, you did what God wanted. He just had something bigger in mind than you did.

Hard Work

You know you ought to pray. But most of the time you're just going through the motions. It's become sheer drudgery. You pray, "Bless so-and-so," but your heart isn't in it. Sometimes you wonder whether you should keep doing it at all. At other times you wonder if you're doing it all wrong. Should prayer be such hard work?

Many times prayer is a drudgery because of a misunderstanding of what it's all about. Prayer is not, "Now I fold my hands and close my eyes." Prayer is an inner dialogue with your best friend. If prayer is going to be enjoyable, it will be because you realize that Jesus is the best friend you've ever had. Jesus is a living friend, a true risen person.

You learn to know your friends gradually — you build up the friendship and finally something beautiful comes. Then you *want* to tell your friend what you're doing and ask him or her to share your life. And you want your friend to do the same with you.

When you get even a smidgen of this kind of friendship going with Jesus, then you're on the road to a beautiful prayer life.

Another reason prayer is drudgery is because people have never gotten to the hard part of commitment where they say, "Okay, Lord, I want to do what you want me to do." Instead, they say, "Here's what I want you to do for me, God." That's not the basis of true conversation with a living God. To pray, to really pray, means we have to pray like Jesus in the Garden of Gethsemane (Luke 22:39-44) and say, "I honestly want to do what you want me to do, God." At times after you've done that you say, "Why did I ever do that?" But once you really make that commitment to God, prayer can become a joy.

> **Prayer is not, "Now I fold my hands and close my eyes." Prayer is an inner dialogue with your best friend.**

Nobody's Out There

You're praying when suddenly the doubt shoots across your mind: "What am I doing? This is foolish. I'm just talking to myself. There's nobody out there listening." The doubt undermines your confidence and enjoyment of praying. How can you be sure you're not talking to yourself when you pray?

I wish I had a good answer to that one but I don't. I know what it's like. You stop your prayers and think, "Good grief, what a childish creature I am. Am I a birdbrain? Have I turned off all logic and moved simply into the realm of fantasy?" That flash comes to you, but is it right? Well, I don't think it is.

I don't have a positive proof that God actually hears, unless, of course, I pray so much I really do have contact with the Lord. Even then, I can't even explain it to anyone, can't prove it. I couldn't package it and put it in someone else's soul.

Now, some people feel they can prove God is listening. They say they know God is listening because they get answers to their prayers.

But I have some problems with that. I believe you can concentrate on something, put your mind on it and get it. I know a guy who is a multimillionaire. He could care less about God, but everything he puts his head to turns out money. Does that mean God likes him? No. There is a fact, I believe, that focusing hard on something brings it about. But that doesn't make it prayer.

Because what happens when I pray and I don't get answers? Does that mean I didn't get through to God? Actually, I got through to God and, going ahead of me, he closed the door for my own good. For me to say, "I prayed and got an answer; therefore God is real" leaves me in a dilemma. Because then I sometimes have to say, "I prayed and *didn't* get an answer; therefore God *isn't*." The counteraction to doubting whether God is listening is trusting God, believing that there really is a God who cares just the way Jesus said. Either Jesus was right or he was wrong. I bet he was right.

Phony

When you get in a group prayer, you keep thinking it's a big phony situation. One person will pray just perfectly, and then the next person will top that, and pray the most spiritual-sounding prayer there could ever be. Either you feel terrible, because you doubt you could ever be as spiritual as those people are, or you begin to think the whole deal is phony.

This is why any group prayer has to be

structured to allow time for silent prayer and to let people not pray if they don't feel they can. It's very embarrassing for some folks to pray out loud, and other people can't do anything but get more phony because they don't know any other way. Whenever we begin to try to sound spiritual, we end up with a pretty phony prayer. Prayer is friendship with the Lord. When I hear the kind of prayer that says, "Oh God, I beseech you . . . " I feel so bad for the people who have to pray like that. I won't say that "beseeching" God isn't prayer, but there's a better kind of prayer that is like visiting with a friend. You are honest and open, and just say what you're thinking.

A Monotonous Ritual

Your family always has grace before meals. It's the same old thing, time after time — the words become totally memorized. As far as you can see, it's a monotonous ritual that has become a complete waste of time.

Sure, it could be. Let me tell you a beautiful story. I performed the marriage of former President Jimmy Carter's son Jack. In the governor's mansion the night of the wedding rehearsal there were political wheels, plus a lot of nice kids from the University of Georgia where Jack and Judy were going to school. Quite a mix.

Before the buffet Jimmy Carter knocked on a glass and said, "Would you please bow your heads? I'd like to say a prayer." So here

> # Whenever we begin to try to sound spiritual, we end up with a pretty phony prayer.

was his prayer:

"Lord, Ros and I have had *so* many nice meals together, so much fun around the table, and we thank you. We just ask that Judy and Jack might have that kind of fun around their table. . . . " He went on visiting with the Lord about their mealtimes and the mealtimes he hoped Jack and Judy were going to have together.

Let me tell you, it was quite an experience for the people at that rehearsal dinner. This guy was governor of Georgia, but there he was just visiting up a storm with the Lord about mealtime.

You're not going to do that at every meal. My point is, grace doesn't have to be some formal deal like, "Our heavenly Father, Provider, Lord of the Universe. . . . " It can be, "Ros and I, you know, we have so much fun . . . make it that for Jack and Judy." Stretch the rules so that grace becomes a living thing again.

No Discipline

You know you're too disorganized and rushed to ever have any discipline in your life. People have told you that it's good to have a regular time in the morning to pray. But you wonder if you'll ever be able to do it.

I would say the best time to pray is all the time, without ceasing, as the apostle Paul said (1 Thessalonians 5:17). I think he meant that the whole of life, if the inner presence of Christ is turning you on to everything, is going to be a conversation with the Lord.

But beyond that, Martha and I find that we pray best if we have a quiet time set aside for prayer. It could be morning for some, evening for others. We'll run through the day with him, just checking through all the events and giving them to him.

I also pray throughout the day. I have little cues. When the phone rings, I pray that I'll be able to serve whoever is on the line. Or when I look at my watch, I'll say, "Thanks for time, Lord. Help me to use it for you." If the doorbell rings, that's a cue to pray for the person I'm going to meet in a second. Whenever I hear a siren, I try to think of the people who need help right that second and pray for them.

Anger is also a cue. When I get angry at somebody I try to remember to pray. I'm not saying I've got this together completely. But I am moving in the right direction, trying to remember to turn my anger over to God. Just the other day I got angry at a guy in the airport. Man, was he rude. I wanted to hit him right in the mouth. So, I said, "Lord, this guy is really bugging me. Help him. He's got problems. He needs help. And so do I."

Discipline in prayer takes time to develop. But it's worth the effort.

Someone's Watching, Someone Cares

Ed Lallo

Your new father knows what is best for you and has spared no expense to make sure your life is everything it can be. And to demonstrate just how much he values you, he gave the costliest gift imaginable — he gave the life of his only son. That is how important he considers your life with him. His concern and his caring leave nothing to chance.

S.K. Wong

Without God

Life on this planet is just a happy accident, a cosmic fluke. You are born, you live, you die. On the timetable of the universe you're just a momentary pinpoint spark; too brief to be noted. So, live while you can. Enjoy yourself because this is all there is; when you're dead there's nothing but a long, dark night.

With God

Every living thing on this big blue marble gliding through space was created out of the word of the Master Artist, fixed in its place for a purpose. You, too, have a purpose — one that goes far beyond this temporary life. God, the creator, wants to show you your purpose; he wants you to know him as he knows you — personally, intimately, lovingly. He wants you to be with him in perfect peace now and forever.

Without God

All religion is salve for man's uneasy conscience, a lubricant for social progress. You have to forget about some all-seeing, all-knowing supernatural force and just get on with business. If the world is in a mess it's up to us to fix it and make it right — all the best and most noble intentions won't help. You have to learn that you are responsible for your own life, your own heaven or hell — it's whatever you make it.

With God

There is someone who cares what happens to you and to your world. He is closer than a brother and wants to help you grow and become all that you can be, all that you were ever meant to be. Jesus listens when you speak to him, he hears your deepest thoughts, your innermost longings, and he wants you to know that no matter what happens he will be with you. Your struggles are not in vain — he already has prepared a place for you, and a reward beyond description.

David Kreider

Without God	Jesus was a good man and a great teacher. He pointed to a better way to live — the same way that Buddha, Mohammed, Confucius, and other enlightened men have done. These men, and others like them, arise in every age to bring a message of hope and love for their time, helping mankind evolve to its full potential.
With God	Jesus distinctly set himself apart from any other man who ever lived. He was killed for his teaching by the religious establishment of his day, yet he rose again to live forever. No other leader of any of the world's religions has done that, or ever will. His teaching is not merely a message of hope and love, it is the cure for a death-dealing disease: sin. He alone has the power to save men from sin and death because he conquered both.
Without God	There are no absolutes — whether you're right or wrong depends on the situation you're in. Actually, anything can be justified if the circumstances demand it. People should not be blamed for things they do when the situation is beyond their control — you have to do what you think is right at the time. No one has the authority to sit in judgment over anyone else.
With God	Jesus has the authority to sit in judgment over all. He was subjected to the same pressures and temptations as any man and never gave in. He is a true judge, and he is also a friend who is desperately concerned that you learn to live the right way. His laws must be obeyed, but because he is infinitely more concerned with creating new people than with punishing offenders, he stands ready to forgive every mistake. And because he knows how hard it is he has given his Spirit to help you make it through.

Your True Identity

A group of researchers discovered a remarkable fact about the human brain: its ability to filter out a single important word from oceans of nonsense. They placed volunteers at tables in crowded coffee shops and cafeterias where conversation in the air created a pleasant, but meaningless, buzz. The subjects happily rejected the static chatter until one precise word was used. Instantly, they became alert, their pulses quickened, they stopped and listened intently. The word? Their names. Their brains filtered out all the droning noise except the one piece of information important to them, their names.

That really isn't surprising when you think about it. Everyone reacts the same way; you can't help it. Your name is the special tag that separates you from everyone else on this crowded planet. It registers you as a human being, one out of countless millions. All the impressions you give out to your friends — your looks, your personality, your jokes and quirks and tastes — in their minds are lumped together under your name. No one else has precisely the same combination of traits; your name is the trademark for a unique, nonreproducible product: you.

For the orphans on the Orphan Train, those nameless, homeless, vagabonds, receiving a new name meant that they had found a home at last. Of course, there were a multitude of changes to struggle through — to thrust a bunch of scruffy, independent, street-wise kids into the heart of country life in rural America would create a mountain of problems large and small. But the benefits far exceeded any problems. For along with their new names the orphans received a new family and new identities as members of that family.

That's how it is when you become a Christian: you are adopted by a new father; you receive a new name — his name. And every person who becomes a Christian receives a new identity. "When someone becomes a Christian he becomes a brand new person inside. He is not the same anymore. A new life has begun!" (2 Corinthians 5:17, Living Bible).

With your new identity as a Christian you receive a new start, and automatically you get new opportunities to grow, to change, to become the person you were meant to be. The next few chapters will explore that process of growth and change as you begin to discover your new identity, and begin using your new name as a member of God's own family.

Swinging Free

Most of us look at growth as something that just happens — an unavoidable by-product of life. You start out small and if you stick around long enough you get bigger. Nothing to it.

But growth is hard work. Not an idle pursuit at all, it involves change. Have you ever tried to change? If you're shy, how do you stop being shy? You know how to carry on a conversation, but around other people you freeze up. And later you kick yourself for not being able to say all the things you knew you could have said. But you can't just talk yourself out of being shy. Will power alone won't change you.

If it's that hard to change even a little thing like being shy, how do you change in the big ways? Do you just wait around for something to happen? Tim Stafford found trying to change was a lot like climbing a mountain.

most of my rock climbing has been on small cliffs you could climb in five or ten minutes. But a close friend who really knows how to climb took me to Yo-semite Valley once. We climbed an all-day climb known as Royal Arches Direct. It was an easy climb for him, but a bruising, terrifying wall of granite for me.

Most of the time I was balanced on nubbins of rock thinner than my little finger, or trying to scramble up the cliff by jamming my fingers into a crack and gumming at the rock with my boots. My muscles were turning to water. My hands and wrists were scratched and bleeding. And I kept thinking, "What will I do when we have to turn back?"

Then we got to the pendulum. A pendulum is what it sounds like: you fasten the rope high above you on the cliff, then climb down, dangle on the end of the rope and try to swing across rock you couldn't otherwise climb. Planting your feet against the cliff, you lean out against the rope and into space (an awful sensation), and half skitter, half run across the face of the cliff. You lunge at a spot you can grab onto. If you don't make it you swing helplessly back and try again.

When everyone's gone across, you pull the rope after you. From then on, there's no going back. You've crossed a section of cliff you could never cross without a rope to swing on — and the rope is now loosely coiled at your feet. There's only one way to go: up.

by TIM STAFFORD

Robert McQuilkin

45

Robert McQuilkin

When we pulled in that rope, my heart beat very fast. What if we came to something I couldn't handle? I was trapped on the cliff. Before we committed ourselves by pulling in the rope, I asked my partner: was he very sure I could handle this? He was sure. So I

When there was no way back, when it was just me, the rope and the rock, you'd think the pressure would bother me.

went on fearfully.

But amazingly, that fear didn't last long. Instead, I found myself falling into the beautiful, silent rhythm of climbing. And I found myself enjoying it despite the risks.

The pendulum had been the turning point. Before, part of me hadn't been committed. I held back mentally, thinking about the possibility of going back, wondering when the cliff might become too difficult. But after the pendulum that option didn't exist. I was totally committed to the climb.

I believe I climbed better as a result. I know I enjoyed myself more. In fact, when we finally scrambled up over the edge of the cliff, I was sorry the climb was over.

Taking the Risk

Thinking it over later, I realized it hadn't worked the way you might suppose. You'd think I'd be more relaxed as long as there was a way back — a safe escape. When there was *no* way back, when it was just me, the rope, and the rock, you'd think the pressure would bother me. But it worked just the opposite. The moments of decision leading up to the pendulum were the worst. After they were over the fun began.

That seems to be a general rule of life. You are most miserable when there's a risk coming up. The anticipation can kill you. But once you've committed yourself, gone in over your head, swung out on the rope, the fun begins.

It happens outside sports, too. For instance, if you're shy, asking someone out can be agonizing. But where's the pain? Usually *before* you've committed yourself to doing it. Once you're talking to the girl, saying the words, you're involved. If it's going to hurt, it'll hurt any moment. But it doesn't. You've swung on the pendulum, and you are over on the other side. The fun begins.

Friendship is the same. Generally, you become close to someone by opening up your feelings to that person. You reveal something important — some fear, some weakness — and take a risk that the friend might not understand — might not even care. It can be terrifying — especially that heart-stopping instant when you open your mouth to say it. But you put your weight on the rope, you swing out . . . and the first thing you know, you've reached the other side. You've taken the risk, and the fun begins.

Maybe that is obvious. Naturally, life involves risk, you say. It's something everyone knows.

The trouble is, it's not something everyone practices. When was the last time your heart was in your mouth, and you risked something you weren't sure of . . . weren't sure of at all?

Most people are concerned with playing it safe. It's a way of thinking that goes deep: "Don't do anything stupid. Don't let anyone laugh at you. Don't get on a fanatical kick. If in doubt, stay out."

Most people avoid risks. And because they play it safe, they miss all the fun of being really involved . . . of being a little over their heads and coming out all right. They end up hanging at the end of the rope, wanting to pendulum but unsure of the safety — and miserable as a result.

It's interesting, in light of that, to note one of Jesus' statements. It's repeated more than any other of his in the Bible: "The man who tries to save his life will lose it. The man who gives up his life will find it."

In other words, if your biggest worry is your own security, you'll end up losing. There is no safety in playing safe.

When Jesus gathered his disciples, they faced that kind of "pendulum" risk. My climbing partner said, "Come on across." It was all or nothing; I couldn't hang in the middle. And Jesus said, "Follow me." It didn't matter whether the disciples he called were wearing warm clothes at that moment, or whether they had some other business to attend to first. "Follow me," he said. And he meant "now."

They followed. They left their homes and their work, taking all the risks that Jesus might be crazy or a hopeless idealist. Why? Because unless they took the risks they were never going to discover all the things Jesus had for them.

That is the risk of faith. It isn't reckless. It isn't like putting faith in something absurd: jumping off the cliff and hoping air resistance will stop you.

Swinging Free

Faith is more like my pendulum on Royal Arches Direct. I trusted the rope, and most of all I trusted my partner's word when he said I would be able to handle the climb.

Faith trusts God, and what he has said. He has promised to take care of people who lean totally on him.

But no matter how much you want to trust, you have to get to that one terrifying moment when you lean on the rope, swing across and realize there's no way back. It *is* a risk, and it *is* frightening.

When I became a Christian I felt that moment of risk. I prayed, and began to put my weight on God. It was frightening, in a thrilling way, because up until then I'd been playing it safe, leaning on the lie that I was smart enough and good enough to settle my own problems. And now I had put my weight on God and swung off those "securities."

That pendulum feeling keeps surfacing. It comes whenever I tell someone "I'm a Christian." If that person doesn't know I make that claim, I get a kind of false security from drifting anonymously in the crowd. But when I tell him I claim God is real, and real in my life, those securities are gone. I've swung into space. God had better be real in the way I live — and I have to trust God to make that happen.

I felt I was swinging out on the pendulum again not long ago, when I decided I had to love one guy I didn't like. I'd been justifying the way I talked about him to myself, massaging my ego with the fact that "I'm not any worse than anyone else." But I came to the

because I felt exposed. What if God didn't give me that love? I had only his word to cling to.

This is where the Spirit of God comes in. God has promised us that his Spirit will be with us to give us the strength we need to do what he requires. When you begin your relationship with God, he is not content to be a distant friend — someone you send postcards to from time to time, or a relative you phone once in awhile when you think about it and the rates are cheap. Now, a partnership has formed between you. In that partnership, you swing out in faith and he supports you; he understands your strengths and weaknesses and comforts you when you need it. It is a continuous, nonstop arrangement.

As long as you insist on relying on your own power, ignoring God's, you will always be limited in what you can do and what kind of person you can become. But when you begin to turn to God and ask for his power, you begin to do things you were incapable of. God has the power you need. He wants to use it — and he wants to use it *with you*, as a partner. There is no other way — he won't roll over you like a steamroller.

Of course, trusting God to support you that first time is scary. No beginning climber likes to leave solid earth and trust the rope. No one wants to leave himself completely behind and lean on Jesus alone. If you are like everyone else who's ever had to make the choice of "swinging free" of past props, you wonder if there isn't a way to sort of do it halfway.

But there is no way. You cannot avoid that thrilling, fantastic instant when you finally push off and swing free. Only after that can you really climb.

point where I knew God wasn't going to let me live with that kind of rationalizing. I had to swing free of those ego props and grope for the solid love God could give me for him. It was a thrilling and frightening experience

One Small Step

The Chinese have a saying: the longest journey starts with one small step. Sometimes the distance from where we are to where we want to be is so vastly overwhelming it discourages us from even starting on the journey. And the work it takes to grow and change sometimes dwarfs our sternest intentions. Yet, it isn't the huge expanse we have to conquer, it's just that first small step.

She knew when she awoke that things couldn't go on the way they had. Perhaps it was the grayness of the sky, the sameness of the announcer's voice over the clock radio, the same bustle in the kitchen below. . . .

Mechanically Marlene climbed out of bed and groped to the bathroom where she stepped on the scales. A half pound more instead of less. She'd been dieting, supposedly, for six weeks, had lost three pounds and gained back two. The story of her life. It wasn't anything so serious as drugs or promiscuity or failing in school. It was the accumulation of small, everyday things that she felt she could tolerate no longer.

There were footsteps in the hall, and someone pounded on the door.

"C'mon, Mar, I got to brush my teeth! I'll miss the bus!"

"For heaven's sake, I just got in here!" Marlene's voice was shrill. She threw open the door with a scowl on her face, glaring at 13-year-old Rusty, who pushed by her and turned on the water in the sink.

Marlene went back to her room and sat down on the bed. If she'd gotten up sooner instead of listening to the radio for twenty minutes, she would have been out of the bathroom by the time Rusty needed it. And then there was her sister to struggle with. Every morning the same old hassle, the same problems, the same grayness, the same sameness . . . on and on and on. . . .

She looked up and caught her reflection in the mirror — blondish hair, slightly plump face, medium shape — same expression, same Marlene.

She was quiet at breakfast. She always was, but this morning it was a different quiet, as though a small seed had been planted the moment she saw herself in the mirror.

"Want the comics?" her father asked, leafing through the newspaper.

"No. Not this morning," Marlene an-

by PHYLLIS NAYLOR

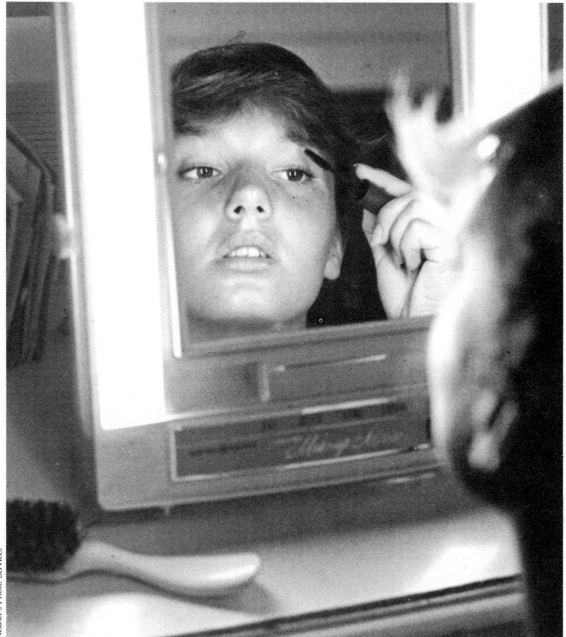

swered, absorbed in the feeling that something was going to happen. Something just *had* to.

"Don't forget to pick up your skirt at the cleaners," her mother called after her as Marlene left for school. But Marlene scarcely heard.

> **It had been such a beautiful moment, and Marlene had walked home in a swirl of snowflakes, singing carols with the others and feeling the joy of aliveness.**

Down the steps, across the wet sidewalk. It was the first day of the month, she remembered suddenly. A new beginning, maybe?

She remembered another first of the month — January 1st. New Year's Day. The youth group at church had held a meeting instead of a party, and as the first few minutes of the new year crept in on them, each of them silently dedicated himself or herself again to God. It had been such a beautiful moment, and Marlene had walked home in a swirl of snowflakes, singing carols with the others and feeling the joy of aliveness. Knowing Jesus personally could be so great. How did it happen that she slipped back so quickly into the old routine — the old habits — the old way of behaving that

made others dislike her at times? She even disliked herself.

Hadn't she always been a Christian? Hadn't she been raised in the church by Christian parents and hadn't she patterned her life after the teachings of Christ? Shouldn't she be able to sail through each day in joy and anticipation, saying and doing the right thing at the right moment?

Instead, there was the constant bickering with Rusty and her sister, her fury at her mother's nagging, her chronic envy of one of the girls at school, her tendency to make remarks that really hurt. Sometimes it seemed as though she was unable to do even the simplest of things, such as diet off a few more pounds, or arrange her time better on Saturdays. Each evening she prayed for guidance and support, and each morning the same trivial troubles faced her all over again. And yet, as she walked to school on this morning in the gray damp, something made her feel that perhaps there was a change in the wind.

She knew for sure that something was about to happen when she walked in the door at school and saw Jennifer Collins coming toward her down the corridor. In another ten seconds they would pass.

Jennifer had everything a girl could want — looks, clothes, money, even her own car — and to top it off, she was kind. People gravitated around her because she treated them well, and it had always seemed like just too much for Marlene to bear. Girls like Jennifer were supposed to be witches underneath — all the novels said so, and though Marlene watched her constantly, she could discover no serious flaws. So she disliked her all the more. Whenever they passed in the hall, Marlene either looked the other way or said a tight, "Hi." The same reluctant greeting. . . .

And suddenly, on this morning as Jennifer approached, Marlene knew the only way to say something different was to say something different. Just open her mouth and do it. With a tremendous effort she forced her lips into a smile and said, actually said, "Hi, Jennifer. I like your boots. They go well with that dress."

Jennifer gave her a surprised smile. "Why thanks, Marlene."

A few seconds at the most, and it was over, yet Marlene felt exhilarated, as though she had climbed Mt. Everest. It was a small battle, but she had won. She wasn't fighting Jennifer, she was fighting herself.

There was something about Jennifer's warm smile that encouraged her. It felt good saying something friendly, but could she keep it up? Marlene didn't know. All she knew was that at that moment she had found the courage to say something generous to someone she envied.

Lunch time. Another battle. However strong she thought she was, Marlene knew that in reality she could be ruled by a single piece of blueberry pie or a glazed doughnut. She stood in line in the cafeteria, mentally figuring out the calories in a bowl of soup and a glass of iced tea. No, she couldn't do it. Her stomach would rumble all through Algebra II, and she'd stop off on the way home and load up with pizza. She would go on forever being somewhat overweight — the same Marlene — cheeseburger, french fries, and milk.

As she reached the counter, however, her eyes caught the calendar on the wall — the first of the month — a new day. All right, she would order one less thing than usual. That much she could do.

"Cheeseburger and milk," she requested. She closed her eyes as she moved past the desserts and on to the cashier. She did it. Another battle won. A small one.

The way to change behavior is to change behavior. She smiled to herself as she sat down in algebra class and opened her note-

However strong she thought she was, Marlene knew that in reality she could be ruled by a single piece of blueberry pie or a glazed doughnut.

book. You can't just *wish* that you could do something differently — you have to do it! Even if it's only a small step. So simple! Why hadn't it worked before?

She was feeling good as she walked home from school. Her step was brisk and her head high. She quickened her steps as she passed the Pizza Shack, and for one awful moment almost turned and went back. But she went on.

"Did you remember to pick up your skirt at the cleaners?" asked her mother when she heard her come in. "I thought you said you'd do it on your way home and save yourself a trip!"

"So I'll take a little walk!" Marlene said impatiently. "Is that so awful?" She stopped,

Gregg Lewis

remembering. "Anything I can pick up for you on the way over?"

There was surprise in her mother's voice. "Well . . . a gallon of skim at Thompson's, maybe."

"Will do. See you later."

It wasn't so easy, however, with Rusty. After dinner, she had one of the worst fights with her brother she ever had.

"Good grief, what happened to my pastels?" she cried, going into the den where her artist chalk was broken in pieces.

"They dropped," Rusty said uncomfortably.

"What do you mean, *they* dropped! You dropped them!" Marlene shrieked. "Look at them! Every single stick is broken! And my sketches are scattered all over the place!"

"The wind must have blown your sketches around," Rusty yelled back, leaping out of his chair and going to the door of the den to see for himself. As he did so his foot stepped on one of the sketches on the floor, leaving a big footprint on the face of a little girl.

In blind fury, Marlene grabbed his hair, her nails digging into his scalp. Rusty yelled and swung at her. Like two caged animals they tore at each other till their father's voice brought their scrapping to a sudden halt.

"Marlene, you're sixteen, not three! Aren't you kids ever going to grow up?"

Tears welled up instantly in Marlene's eyes. "Look what he did!" she cried. "My whole portfolio is scattered around the room!"

"I didn't do it!" Rusty yelled again. "I might have dropped your chalk, but I didn't have anything to do with the papers!"

"OK, Rusty, get your money and pay for the chalk," their father said. "Then do you suppose I could have an hour's peace?"

Marlene lay face down on her bed. She had not only failed this one, she'd failed miserably. It seemed to negate all the other little successes of the day. A ridiculous, hair-pulling free-for-all! *I can't do it*, she wept. *God, I can't do it!* In the silence that followed, she almost expected to hear the roll of thunder and a voice from out of the clouds. Instead, Rusty's half-hesitant twang came from the doorway.

"Here's the ten bucks, Mar. Listen, I'm sorry about that footprint on your sketch."

Marlene reached for a tissue and sat up, avoiding Rusty's eyes. "That's OK," she mumbled. "It wasn't one of my better sketches."

Rusty noticed her red eyes and hung on, wanting to make up. "You may not play volleyball so good, but you sure can pull hair," he said finally.

Marlene had to smile. "Well, that's the last time I'm going to do it. I may scratch or kick you in the shins, but I won't pull hair."

"Hey, that's real great of you," said Rusty, and they both laughed.

Marlene sat at her desk, working on her history assignment. Her mind wandered, and she noticed that she had scribbled "Joyful, yes — easy, no" in the margin. Maybe that's what being a Christian was all about. Whoever said it was easy? All this time she had supposed that Christianity would automatically make her say and feel and do the right thing, without any effort, any sign of a struggle. Now she knew she would be struggling all her life. Could she do it?

Yes, but not all at once. She could not change her feelings overnight, but she could change her behavior, even if only one small change each day. There would be days she would fail horribly, she knew. But she wouldn't let them serve as excuses for not trying again.

100% Solution

Sometimes I feel like I'm being eaten alive. Yes, stripped to the bone by problems. I don't have any big, overwhelming disasters, or disabling handicaps — just the everyday, ordinary problems we all face. But sometimes I feel that everything is ganging up on me and I'll go out of my mind if the problems don't leave me alone.

What kind of problems? The car won't start in the morning and it makes me late . . . I'm on the outs with one of my best friends because of something stupid I said . . . I owe money on my stereo and I haven't got it . . . the work is piling up and I don't have an extra minute to get anything done . . . I gain back the three pounds I worked so hard to take off on my diet . . . the list is nearly infinite.

I know there's nothing in any of those problems that can't be worked out. I also know that when I do finally rid myself of one problem, another will spring up like a weed to take its place. They never seem to end. Yet, my church has always told me that by praying, believing, and worshiping faithfully, I would be free. Apparently, that's not true — no matter how hard I pray or how much I believe, problems still come up — praying doesn't start my car or pay my bills. Am I doing something wrong?

Clearly, the problem of *problems* is deeper than I first suspected. We are all led to believe that our problems have solutions — most of them do, that's true, but we focus so much attention on how to solve the individual problems that crop up, we don't realize there's more involved.

For example, in high school my problems centered around school, friends, going out, self-image, appearance, popularity, etc. Having acne or not ever being asked out were real problems. Serious problems. They certainly created as much anxiety, frustration, and worry as any so-called "major" problem.

Whenever I complained about my problem (whatever it might be) someone (usually an adult) would say, "You haven't got it so bad. Just think of all the starving children in Africa!" True, by comparison I didn't have much to complain about. Still, the feelings connected with my problem were as traumatic as the Africans' — I was sure of that. Thinking about other miserable people didn't help at all. If anything, it only made matters worse by making me feel guilty on top of everything else.

Getting older was certainly no cure. I lost weight, my face cleared up, my parents started trusting me, I got out on my own — all the things I wanted. But the problems didn't go away, they just changed. As soon as I got out on my own, my job became much more important. When it wasn't going well, it opened up a whole new area of problems. What about getting married? Raising a family? Paying bills? The teenage problems merely gave way to adult problems (which I strongly suspect will give way to old-age problems).

That is a chilling thought — there is no freedom from problems. But it brings with it a cool logic: if problems are a natural part of life, then having

by STEVE LAWHEAD

problems is normal (and having *no* problems is abnormal). Well that, at least, was a thought I could relax with. I was normal after all. And then an answer suggested itself to me; most of us are handling our problems the wrong way.

Like most people, I suppose, I have always carried around in my mind the idea that "if only _____, then my problems would be over." Fill in the blank: "If only I had more friends, if only I wasn't overweight. . . . " I was always looking for some supreme problem solver.

My goal in getting free from problems had been to search out a way to get rid of all problems once and for all (by getting more money, having more friends, finding a new job, etc.). My goal should have been to learn how to handle problems. I had always seen life as a set of individual problems that required individual solutions. Instead, problems are a condition, like being human. No matter what state I am in, problems will follow me the rest of my life. To some that might seem an unduly pessimistic thought. It's really not. It's a freeing thought.

Life is a forest of problems: you won't ever be free by handling them like single trees, one at a time. To be completely free, you have to have a way of dealing with the entire forest — once you do, the individual problems can't ever bother you as much.

I'm sure that if God wanted to, he could solve all my problems, present and future, with a wave of his hand. But would that do me any good? Most likely not. I would be like a hothouse plant, delicate and comfortable, but unable to survive outside of my narrow environment. It would be much better to be a plant that could take the extremes of the hottest summer and the coldest winter, lightning and thunder and rain; to take it all and still thrive.

But in facing all the diverse elements of life, God has not left us defenseless. He has attacked the heart of every problem and given us a way to defuse all of them. He has given us his love.

God's overwhelming love for us is mentioned many places in the Bible. In the New Testament, Paul shows us the power of this love. "For I am convinced that nothing can ever separate us from his love. Death can't, and life can't. The angels won't, and all the powers of hell itself cannot keep God's love away. Our fears for today, our worries about tomorrow, or where we are — high above the sky, or in the deepest ocean — nothing will ever be able to separate us from the love of God . . . " (Romans 8:38-39, Living Bible). Paul was convinced of God's love as a fact. Down in the center of his being he knew God's love and trusted it completely. That trust gave him a solid core that nothing could ever shake; it even allowed him to rejoice in times of trouble. And Paul was no stranger to trouble: jail, shipwrecks, beatings, lynch mobs out to kill him and finally execution as a criminal of the state. Yet, none of Paul's problems caused him to despair. He never doubted his ultimate security.

That same security Paul had is available to each one of us. Simply, it is trusting God's love for us, and knowing that whatever happens he is there to call on and he will share his strength with us. It is taking me a long time to learn that, and I'm still learning.

Sin

You can decide to "swing free" and take that "first small step" leading to a significant change in your life. But something keeps getting in your way. It's that ever-present problem with the old-fashioned name: sin. When you least expect it sin spins its sticky web to confound your best intentions. Philip Yancey offers some potent thoughts on disarming the Christian's chief enemy.

Alexander Solzhenitsyn, the Nobel prize-winning Russian author, taught me one important fact about sin. He learned it while spending eight years inside a Siberian concentration camp because of a cutting remark he had made about Stalin.

To the Russian government, there were clearly two classes of people: first, the dangerous, evil people who had to be locked behind bars to protect the Russian people. Then there were the rulers and guards: honest, dependable men who were given the noble task of keeping society pure.

Inside the camp, though, everything looked very different. To Solzhenitsyn and his friends, the guards were the villains. After all, they locked him up without a fair trial, jerked him away from his family, and forced him to live in misery. Every day he was given only eight ounces of bread and warm mush; yet he was required to work long hours without pay throughout the Siberian winter. Guards were mean, inconsiderate, even sadistic. Prisoners, though, stuck together. They could be counted on.

Sin tends to create barriers like that — different ways of looking at people. In the sixties, Northerners looked down on Southerners because they were supposedly less tolerant of black people, therefore sinful. Meanwhile, other countries looked down on the United States because we were bogged down in a questionable war.

Sometimes Christians try to use sin as a barrier to separate themselves from others. They tend to snub certain groups, judging them as inferior. Yet, when you boil it down, the chief difference between the Christian and others is only that Christians admit they are sinners who need God's help. They acknowledge that they are painfully like, not better than, all other people.

Actually, the one thing most true about sin

by PHILIP YANCEY

Mimi Forsyth

is that it unites us. We're not all crooks, perverts, or murderers. But we all are selfish, proud, and uncaring.

Solzhenitsyn came to realize that, even in the bleakness of his concentration camp. Here is what he wrote: "It was only when I lay there on rotting prison straw that I sensed within myself the first stirrings of good. Gradually, it was disclosed to me that the line separating good and evil passes, not through states, nor between classes, nor between political parties either, but right through every human heart, and through all human hearts. So, bless you, prison, for having been in my life."

For Our Sakes

If you ask a friend to define sin, he may say something like this: "Oh, that's easy. It's having a good time doing what you're not supposed to do."

I think of the image of God as a finger-wagging librarian roaming the corridors of earth saying "Shhhhh" to all happy people. But it doesn't fit. God, after all, created such things as a taste for rich foods, a voicebox that allows laughter, a beautiful shape for the human body. When he created those things he announced they were good.

However, exploiting those good things doesn't necessarily lead to "a good time." Visit a prison and ask a sex pervert if he enjoys what he does. He'll likely break down and cry, mumbling something about how trapped he feels, how he has a craving that's never satisfied. Ask an alcoholic — you'll get the same response.

God gave us trees; we turn them into clubs and beat each other. He gave us food; we engorge it and grow fat while half the world goes hungry. He gave us sex; we use it to satisfy ourselves even when we know we're hurting other people. Is it right to blame God for these things?

I used to think that God's primary reaction to my sin was to want to punish me. But I have come to see his reaction is much more loving. He wants to *free* me from sin, for *my* sake. God knows I can have a good time on this earth boozing it up, messing around with girls, making fun of other people, getting rich. But he has in mind a much higher calling. He wants me to be good.

Being good seems very boring until I think of people who truly are good. There was one teacher in my high school who stood out. He was not threatening; any student felt free to air a gripe with him. He was completely fair, even when it came to grading. And he cared so much about biology that he turned down a much higher-paying job so he could try to infect others with his own excitement about it.

All of us feel a touch of goodness sometimes, a longing for something better. C.S. Lewis described it as "a scent of a flower we have not found, the echo of a tune we have not heard, news from a country we have never yet visited." God has promised us that life with him is "life in all its fullness," more rich and satisfying than any other kind.

Sin has its own immediate rewards — but each of those rewards is a mere stumbling block to the better rewards God intended for us. He wants to free us from sin, not for his sake, but for *our* sakes.

A Way Out

Sin is really our problem, not God's. He created each of us with a built-in mechanism for knowing when we're sinning — our conscience bothers us. If we want to be free from the turmoil of an offended conscience, we have to be free from sin because there is no way to be free from our conscience; it's as much a part of us as is our stomach. But God offers the only solution to this problem and Christians know what it is: forgiveness.

Once a good friend of mine told me why he had never become a Christian. "It's because they're always so guilty," he said. "They go around with their heads down, and backs bent like they're carrying an enormous burden."

I felt like laughing out loud, and crying at the same time. Maybe the Christians he knew went around feeling guilty; if so, that was painfully sad. Actually, as anyone who has been converted should know, the Christian is the only person who does *not* go around feeling guilty. For Christians, sin is a burden they can put down. They are forgiven.

The really pitiful people are the ones who deny the existence of sin at all. Their consciences never quite give up screeching and they must go through life gnawed by guilt — but unable to do anything about it.

Sometimes I think God uses guilt as a last resort. If we don't obey him, because we don't believe that his way is best, he lets guilt take over, pointing us back whether we feel very obedient or not. Guilt is like a crutch. It's there when we need it, but wouldn't it be much better for us to develop our legs (changing our desires, tastes, and habits to God's will)?

Sin grows up over me like a shell almost overnight. The second I start feeling I've *arrived* — at that second I'm most vulnerable to thinking I don't need God. I like to think of sin as just that — a sign pointing me to God. There's nothing good about sin, and I'm never grateful for it; it stunts my growth. Nevertheless, I must respond when I sin. I can respond by turning to God, allowing him to bathe me and to teach me what is truly good for me. Or, of course, I can respond by greedily clinging to my sin, letting it bubble awhile inside me. I may have my good time, temporarily. But that's all I'll have. In the process I'll lose myself.

There's one last, dangerous aspect to sin: it can prove fatal. If you don't choose Christ, it makes little difference what you do choose. That is, whether you're a crook or a model citizen won't ultimately matter if along the way you have rejected Christ, the only one who can lead you out of sin. G.K. Chesterton put it this way: "There are an infinity of angles at which one falls, only one at which one stands."

Wild, Wicked Rumor

Having a new identity and the freedom to grow and change is great. There is a vitality you feel as a new Christian that makes it seem like you could move mountains on the moon. But what happens when you wake up one morning and the excitement, the warm, rosy glow, is gone? What happens when you just plain don't feel it's working, when you stop feeling like the new person you are and feel like your old self again?

A wild, wicked rumor is floating around that says when a person becomes a Christian, life magically straightens out. All problems melt away, troubles vanish, success leaps to the touch.

The way some people talk, Christians suddenly locate parking places when others can't, they never get sick and they find contact lenses while all about them others are losing theirs. If you're a Christian your pimples clear up. Exams no longer hold the same terrors; with a prayer the facts stick to your brain like bugs on fly paper.

God *can* do miracles, but the fact is, miracles are exceedingly rare. Your Algebra exam is just as hard as your friends', and your contact lens just as hopelessly lost. God doesn't often change your circumstances when you become a Christian. God's new people are not problem-free people.

But the rumor persists. And part of its persistence is no doubt found in the fact that for many people the very act of becoming a Christian is such an emotional high that all problems *do* seem to fade from view. Life looks so much better you think you've found the Promised Land. You feel God's closeness and all doubts vanish like fog before the hot sun. You walk, not quite touching ground, lit by an inner flame of glowing assurance.

Beware: there's danger here. That supercharged emotional high can dissipate, the glow fade. You wake up one morning and it's gone. What do you do? You dredge up all the things God might be angry about, like the times you were goofing around when you could have been praying. Is God punishing you?

The days shuffle by and you feel more and more miserable. Eventually you begin drifting back into your pre-Christian lifestyle, the very thing you vowed you never would do. But it doesn't seem to matter anymore, so you let it slide. You just don't *feel* like a

by STEVE LAWHEAD

Carlos Vergara

Christian.

It happens to all Christians — sooner or later the don't-feel-like-a-Christian blues catch up with you. For a person who's just become a Christian they can be a frustrating letdown — like having the mumps on Christmas. To a Christian of several years, these spiritual blues can make your faith seem old and stale, dried up and withered. Sometimes the spark fades gradually and sometimes it disappears so quickly it seems your heart itself has been torn out. But the effect is the same: that special feeling is gone and seems like it will never return.

Listen: it's natural. The don't-feel-like-a-Christian blues happen to all Christians, young and old; it makes no difference. What does make a difference is how you let them affect you and your relationship with God.

A Common Problem

Kim was the most enthusiastic new Christian in Boise, Idaho. She had become a Christian as a sophomore in high school and for a-while everything was balloons and pinwheels. Then she became depressed. "There must be a reason for feeling the way I do. I must have *done* something really terrible to *feel* this bad," she complained, assuming God was punishing her for some sin by taking away her good feelings.

Ron became a Christian at a Campus Life retreat in Colorado. He expected a small-scale revolution, but he soon found he still felt shy around girls and still had problems at home. "The trouble is *me*," he thought. "I'm not really a Christian because I don't feel any different. Things haven't changed. I'm no good." He began condemning himself.

Both Kim and Ron were wrong. God does not condemn us for not feeling like we think

Christians should feel. And he doesn't punish us by taking away our joy and making us wonder what we did to offend him.

When we do something we know offends God, it often wrecks our happiness. When that happens, getting back those good feelings depends on getting back into communication with him. But you needn't play private detective to discover those "secret sins." If you can't find anything wrong, relax — you're OK. If God has something against you, he'll confront you with it personally. He'll bring it to mind or needle your conscience with it. There's no such thing as a secret sin to God.

And though he wants us to grow closer to him, God does not condemn us for not being the kind of Christian that we think we should be. In fact, he doesn't condemn us at all. Paul, in Romans 8:1, says that God doesn't hold anything against anyone who belongs to Christ. It's a fact. Accept it!

Doug was the captain of his high school football team, as popular as one person could be. When he became a Christian in his senior year he was totally transformed, and the whole school noticed it. He floated around like a hot-air balloon for six months. When he crashed everyone heard the thump. He tried everything he knew to get the good feelings back but nothing worked, so he simply let his faith drift away.

Doug had bought an emotional trip. As long as he was high, he was willing to be a Christian. But as soon as his "kicks" stopped, he dropped out. Doug's problem is a common one, so common many ministers tell new converts that they can *expect* to lose that inner glow. That seems a bit harsh, especially if you are feeling real peace and joy for the first time. But enough people have crashed and abandoned Christianity that it makes a warning necessary. The good feelings are fringe benefits, the "extra special bonus" God gives us.

Being a Christian is not based on *feeling* like a Christian. Jesus lived and died for us. As God's Son, he saved us. That cannot be changed. It would remain the same for all time if *no one* ever felt like a Christian.

Doug should have realized his good feelings wouldn't last forever. Feelings, good or bad, never do. When someone very close to us dies, we may feel as if our world has caved in. But, no matter how bad we felt in the beginning, there soon comes a time when no more tears will come — when we are unable to feel anything. That doesn't mean we haven't lost a loved one, only that our emotions have been disconnected for awhile.

Emotions work the same way in the Christian life. Doug's Christianity hadn't failed him. God hadn't moved away. He was still there with Doug, only Doug couldn't feel it. He shouldn't have given up.

In many ways the Christian life is like getting married. First, there's the ceremony, and then the gifts and the photos. All your friends are present and there's a big wedding cake, and finally the honeymoon. Everything is so wonderful and overwhelming — it's like nothing you've ever experienced. But there comes a day when you have to get back to the business of living.

The alarm clock buzzes you out of deep, peaceful slumber. You mumble and moan, but there is no putting it off. Monday morning has caught you. You shake yourself out of bed, brush your teeth, comb your hair and face the world. There is cooking and cleaning to be done, a home to take care of, and money to earn. You can't live on wedding cake and starry eyes forever.

In your Christian life, as in your married life, there will be bumps to get over and work out. No one is foolish enough to think that just because a person is married, problems don't arise. Why do we expect a new relationship with Christ to be so different?

One of the great things about a marriage relationship is that there is always someone to share those problems and troubles with. The Christian also has someone to help share his or her problems: fellow Christians. Your Christian friends should be the first to know if you are having a rough time. You shouldn't resent them if they suddenly appear to be playing the part of "Super Saint." (Any resentment you feel is probably your own temporary frustration and disappointment.) Talk to them, seek their advice. Don't let the blues cheat you out of some good, close fellowship. The blues can do that; they can isolate you by making everything seem phony and unreal.

Next time the old don't-feel-like-a-Christian blues have you humming in a minor key, remember — Christians will have times when they don't feel anything like Christians. However, in times like those faith is formed, strengthened, and deepened. So give your faith a chance to grow. Don't give up on it just when it seems hollow and vacant. As Joe Bayly said, "Don't forget in the darkness what you have learned in the light."

When you're down, expect the tide to turn. Keep on going, and sooner or later the good feelings will return. Good feelings *do* come back. Maybe like a light in a dark closet that has been turned off for weeks. Maybe like a slow and natural sunrise after a long, dark night.

Rainy Day Feelings

When I asked God to take over my life, I felt good. I will never forget the sense of adventure that the next morning brought. I had a friend in God, a forgiving, loving, wise and comforting father. He had plans for my life. I could talk to him.

But time went by and I discovered that, emotionally, things are not that simple. I could get down, sometimes depressed almost to the point of despair. Talking to God at those times seemed like talking to a wall. The joy was gone.

I thought I must be doing something wrong. I prayed harder, yet felt no change. I searched for sin in my life, yet sometimes found that confession brought no relief. I would try to take my mind off myself and work at helping others or ask friends to pray for me. Sometimes, too, for a reason I could never track down, my feelings would get better by themselves. But I found I could not count on any one technique to make me feel better.

When I felt down and far away from God, some of my friends recommended a new way of praying. Others recommended reading certain passages of Scripture. Yet when these didn't work, what could I do? Investigate other religions? What?

For me, the first key to feeling better was to become a little skeptical about my emotions. Just because I feel bad today doesn't prove I really am especially bad. The fact that yesterday I didn't feel God's presence doesn't prove he wasn't there.

Many times I feel bad because I am very tired, or am going through turmoil and transition. My bad feelings don't prove anything except that I need rest.

Feelings have a way of changing, without reason, good to bad to good to bad again. Feelings are as unpredictable as gremlins. No, I take that back. Over periods of time there *are* broad patterns to feelings, patterns you can predict. But day to day, feelings are as unpredictable as . . . the weather.

I like that analogy. I lived five years in Illinois, where the weather can change faster than anywhere I've ever been. One summer day we'd be sweltering at 95°, the next we might be shivering in a rainy 55°. But whether it was hot or cold, I never doubted that summer was summer. The weather was more or less predictable — you knew that in summer most days would be hot. But you didn't tell the season by reading the weather report. You read the calendar.

Later I lived in California. In my town, near San Francisco, the weather was wonderful. We had blue skies and comfortable temperatures at least two days out of three. But still, on any given day the weather could be rotten. Friends came out to visit us and wondered why all the big talk about California weather — a cold rain drizzled the whole time they were there. Still, I never doubted that I loved it in California, or that the weather was good there. I didn't even doubt it when we endured a

by TIM STAFFORD

two-year drought. Many people were sure that the weather pattern was changing forever (as a few years before they were worried about California falling into the ocean). But I've got friends and relatives who are farmers, and they had learned that droughts come, but they don't last forever. You take whatever measures you can to conserve water, and you wait for the weather to turn. You don't sell your farm and move to Australia.

The fact is that, if you are living as a Christian, you are living in the sphere of God's grace. The climate is good there. There are good days and bad days, and there may be a long drought. It could be, too, that if you're always feeling wet there is a leak in your roof. You ought always to check that possibility of something wrong in your life. Maybe you aren't listening to God. Maybe you have emotional problems that need to be talked out with a counselor. Maybe there are patterns in your life that need to be changed.

But for the most part, you brave bad times the way you brave bad storms. The spiritual weather may be bad for a time, but you never doubt that in God's climate the weather, overall, will be good. God will reappear. You wait, you "weather" the glumness and the emptiness of feeling that God has disappointed you. And as you grow older, you find yourself looking back on the "big storm of '79," smiling at how bad the weather could be. When you stop worrying so much over long winters, it leaves you freer to enjoy the sunny seasons.

Show Me Who You Are

Laura Garza

Your identity is how you represent yourself to the world around you. When God enters your life your identity begins to change. Sooner or later you will see a great difference between your old identity and your new one as a Christian.

Without God

How far you go in life is up to you; you can do whatever you want. The potential lies within you. With hard work, dedication, and determination anything is possible — if you want it bad enough. When you find what you want go after it. No one will give it to you.

With God

Strength and will power are fine for some things, but they are not the answer to all life's quandaries. Jesus said that in order to truly find your life you have to lose it — a contradiction? Not really. He meant that in letting go of your own power, in releasing your selfish ambitions, in emptying your heart of its pride in your own accomplishments — by getting rid of all the things that crowd out God's presence, you make room for him to work. When God can move freely in your life, then you will find yourself.

Without God

Why do I always have to say the wrong thing? I don't mean to hurt people . . . or maybe I do. I guess deep down inside I do. Something in me wants to be soothed at the pain of someone else. But it doesn't work; I don't feel good. I end up hating myself every time, feeling so guilty. There's no escape. I do the very thing I hate, the very thing I promised I would not do. I'm trapped and there is no way out.

With God

The trap has an escape hatch. It's called forgiveness. When God comes into your life sin doesn't automatically fade away. You still sin. But God stands ready to forgive you when you do. He breaks the awful, downward spiral of sin and its load of guilt. All you have to do is ask for his forgiveness and it's yours.

Jean-Claude Lejeune

Without God

All rivers are pretty much alike — good places to fish, to walk along and think, to swim, to park alongside with someone special in the moonlight. But they can change, too. In the springtime they flood and ruin people's basements. School kids drown when they skate out too far on thin ice. Rivers are another reminder that life isn't always smooth, and that the good moments are fleeting.

With God

The river mirrors your own ever-changing emotions. Sometimes violent and dangerous — sometimes calm and reflective, but moving in cycles through its course. Feelings are insubstantial, like water, nothing to base your faith on. God is the bedrock the river rests upon. He never changes. Don't trust your feelings — trust him.

Home Is Where Your Values Are

T hink for a moment about the word home. What does it mean to you? A white frame house with trees in the front yard and a garden in the back — or, maybe a familiar brick third-floor walk-up. The smell of bread baking in the oven when you walk into the kitchen. A Christmas tree with tiny lights warming to a festive holiday mood. Chances are the word home creates some definite pictures in your mind.

But one thing you might not think of right away is your personal outlook — your values, the way you look at the world. Yet this is certainly as much a part of your home as the porch swing, or your dad's old fishing tackle box.

From the very beginning, before you were even able to walk or talk, you began assimilating the habits and lifestyle of your family. Most likely your parents' views on things are your views, their tastes are your tastes. Is chocolate ice cream your dad's favorite dessert? Is it yours? If your mother thinks soap operas are silly, you probably think so, too. In other words, what your family thinks is important, you tend to hold as important also. What motivates your family motivates you.

Of course, you may not exactly mimic your father or mother in everything; you probably even react strongly against some of their views. But along the way you'll absorb much from your family. You may find sooner or later that you've internalized your parents' values: their habits, motives, priorities are now your own.

The exact nature of your home can differ vastly from that of even your closest relative. But some things don't change. Home is where you first learn right from wrong, the importance of helping others, love for one another. Home is where your values are formed.

As a new Christian, you also enter a new home. Since God is the head of this home his values are imparted to all who call him "father." As a member of his home you'll find that some of your old values are being transformed. The more you learn about God, the more you begin to see things his way. A new home means new values.

Naturally, some of your old values will conflict with the new. And why not? Your old values took years to form and they cannot be changed overnight. But you'll begin to see areas where change is needed, and you'll want to change. The following chapters examine what takes place when you enter your new home.

Guest Who Took Over

Exchanging old values for new ones is not like shrugging off an old coat and slipping on a new one. Your values are the very underpinnings of your life, the foundation you've built on. They affect every single thing you do, the way you look at the world. Changing them is a superhuman task that simply cannot be tackled alone. You need Jesus' help.

How does he do it? By storming in and knocking everything over like a bulldozer breaking ground? No, he's very polite. He works quietly in the areas you allow him to. The process is a little like having a guest in — but not an ordinary guest: God himself, the one who made the universe. Imagine what it would be like.

December
Saturday, 6th

Today I made up my mind, I'm going to invite Jesus into my life. Now, I've got a big, rambling, ranch-style life with a lot of rooms. I'm sure I can make him feel at home. I've put new curtains in the guest room and everything's ready. He'll like living with me.

by STEVE LAWHEAD

Sunday, 7th

He arrived just like he said he would; he came right in — added a little class to my life. I'm sure glad I asked him. There may be a few little things to rearrange, but I'm sure we'll get along just fine.

Wednesday, 10th

I found out that he doesn't want to stay in his room all the time. I don't know what to do. I had assumed he would be comfortable there, but he said, "I didn't come here to be a guest. If I'm going to live here, I'd like to see the rest of the house."

Thursday, 11th

Last night I took him to the den. It's one of my favorite rooms, so I thought for sure he would like it. It's a cozy room, not large at all, with deep leather chairs — good for reading and thinking.

He came in with me and started looking around. He went over to the bookshelf and picked up my copy of *Penthouse*. That made me a little nervous, to say the least. Then he went over and looked at the pictures on the wall. He cast a doubtful eye at my gun-and-knife collection, and that did it. He didn't say anything, but I felt pressure to please such an

Wm. Koechling

important guest. I blurted out, "You know, Jesus, I've been meaning to do a little redecorating in here. Perhaps you would like to have a say in it, too?" He replied, "I'd be delighted to help you. But I'm afraid some of these things will have to go."

"Just say the word and they're gone," I told him. What a relief.

Tuesday, 16th

I'd been planning to have him down for a banquet dinner as soon as he settled in. The Lord didn't seem to enjoy it as much as I had hoped he would. Not at first, anyway.

Before dinner, we had some appetizers. Nothing fancy, just some potato chips and onion dip, some cheese crunchies, pretzels, and taco fluffies. We were munching away when he asked me, "What are we having for dinner?"

I told him, "We're having pizza and french fries, a whole can of pork and beans, and for dessert — chocolate-covered doughnuts with raspberry ice cream and marshmallow sauce. Later on we'll have some popcorn and cotton candy, for a snack." I had no sooner read off the menu than I saw him frowning. "Did I leave anything out, Jesus?" I asked him.

"No, not a thing," he laughed. "I couldn't help noticing that everything you were planning on serving was insubstantial junk. Garbage, as food. Where's the meat? Vegetables? Bread? That's what you really need."

"Bu-but," I stuttered, "I like this food. I eat it all the time. It pleases me."

"Look," Jesus said, getting up, "show me where the kitchen is and I'll fix you something that will put meat on your bones. You've been indulging your shallow appetites and desires too long. I think you'll find the change rewarding."

He went in and made the most delicious meal, using the meat and vegetables of God's will and the bread of the Scripture. I must admit it was satisfying. I plan to be eating better now that he is here.

Wednesday, 17th

Tonight after supper I took the Lord into the living room. He liked it at once — called it the fellowship room. He said, "We'll come here every evening for fellowship. We'll talk and pray and really get to know each other well."

I thought it was a terrific idea at the time, so I told him, "That suits me just fine, Lord." And we sat down and had the best talk I can remember having.

Thursday, 25th

Tonight I was heading for the first of two Christmas parties. As I came down the hall I happened to glance through the door of the living room and saw Jesus sitting on the couch. He wasn't reading or anything, just sitting there waiting. I poked my head in the door. "Waiting for somebody?"

"Yes, as a matter of fact, I was waiting for *you*," he said.

"Me?" I asked. I hadn't the faintest idea what he was talking about. "I'm going out to a Christmas party," I told him. Then it hit me. Since our first time together, I had neglected our fellowship time. He had waited for me every evening while I went my merry way. My face turned crimson with embarrassment.

"I'm dreadfully sorry," I said. "Please forgive me for keeping you waiting."

"I forgive you," he said. "Now sit with me, if only a few moments, and we'll pray before you have to leave."

Needless to say, he did most of the praying — I was too ashamed.

Mike Burkey

Monday, 29th

Had the day off today, so I thought I'd spend a few hours puttering around the workshop. Jesus met me at the basement door, just as I was starting down. I figured that, being a carpenter by trade, he would like to see my tools. Indeed, he was impressed with how well-stocked my shop was.

"I am very proud of my workshop," I told him. "I've got the tools and materials you need to do almost anything."

"Wonderful!" Jesus said. He glanced around the basement room and, looking rather disappointed, declared, "I don't see any-thing you've made."

"Well, I made these." I brought out three balsawood airplanes.

"Is that all? I expected a man as well-equipped as you to have done much more than that," he said sadly.

"I like toys, so I make them," I told him frankly. "I don't know how to make anything else. A lot of tools are useless for me, I'm afraid. I've never had the skill to use them."

His face broke into a smile. "You'll learn," he said encouragingly, "because I'll teach you." I've got to say, he does know his business. I'm often amazed at how well things turn out when he is guiding me through the steps. I'm going to learn a lot, I can tell.

Wednesday, 31st

Big party tonight! We're going to bring the new year in right! All my friends will be there and we'll get it on. Happy New Year!!

January
Thursday, 1st

I feel terrible. Last night wasn't a good night and I didn't have any fun. What happened was this:

I was throwing this New Year's shindig in my rec room and most of the guests had arrived. Gossip was making out with Lust on the couch. Arrogance and Envy were playing Ping-Pong and yelling at each other. Drunkenness was standing on top of the TV singing "The Impossible Dream" at the top of his lungs. Depravity, with his obscene jokes and weird sense of humor, was on the way.

Things were just getting wound up for the evening when in walked Christ. I had forgotten all about him. I guess I knew what kind of party it would be, so I just didn't invite him. He looked around with an expression on his face like *I've seen it all before.* He came over and asked me, "You enjoy this kind of thing?"

"Well, it's OK for laughs," I said. My friends were listening to us talk, and I didn't want to hurt their feelings. "But it's nothing

Bob Combs

serious. It's just for fun."

"Is it?" he asked.

"Is it what?" I didn't know what he was talking about.

"Is it fun?" He looked at me hard and I just couldn't lie to him.

"You want to have fun? I invented fun," he told me. "Get rid of these clowns and I'll introduce you to some of my friends."

"Well, not really," I told him. "I used to think so, but not anymore."

"You want to have fun? I invented fun," he told me. "Get rid of these clowns and I'll introduce you to some of my friends. We'll show you what fun is meant to be."

I'm ashamed at what I did next. I turned him off. I just walked away and left him standing there. I ignored him and, after a while, he left.

But my evening was ruined. I didn't enjoy myself at all. I didn't sleep well last night, either. So, I got up early and patched things up with Jesus, and while I don't feel much better about it, he assures me he'll help me get over it.

Friday, 2nd

I was on my way to meet Jesus in the living room this morning when he stopped me in the hall. There was a pained expression on his face and I could see that something was troubling him.

"What's the matter?"

"There's something dead around here," he said. "I can smell it. A rat or something has crawled in and died in your closet."

Panic set in. I knew what was in my closet and I didn't want him to look in there. "Oh, it's probably nothing, Lord," I assured him. "Let's go into the living room and talk."

"I want to talk about what's in your closet," he said. He was firm.

"Well, it's really nothing, uh — just some antiques."

"Antiques?" He said the word and looked right through me, reading my thoughts.

"Yeah, just a few personal things," I said, trying to keep up the deception. "After all, it's none of your business." That was the wrong thing to say for sure. I knew that as soon as I had said it.

He disregarded the comment completely. "You don't expect me to live here with something dead in the closet, do you?" Then he smiled. "I think your 'antiques' are a little moldy and it's time to get rid of them. Let's clean the closet."

"Oh, Lord, I know I should throw them out, but I just can't. I haven't got the strength. Can't you handle it? I'm afraid. I hate to ask, but. . . . "

"Say no more. Just give me the key and I'll do the rest. I don't mind a bit."

He did it all. Cleaned out the hall closet and never once mentioned a word about it. Lately I've been thinking of giving him the deed to this place — giving it all to him. I'm sure he could run it better than I do. What do you think he would say if I asked him?

Adapted from *My Heart, Christ's Home* by Robert Boyd Munger, © 1954 by Inter-Varsity Christian Fellowship, United States of America. Used by permission.

Mind Bind

Sometimes the difference between your old values and the new ones being formed inside you is so radical, and the struggle is so violent, it's like a war. You want to be one way, but you act another.

We talked to Jay Kesler, President of Youth for Christ, about this problem — probably the most common malady among Christians.

I call the feeling "double-mindedness." It feels awful — like the kids on the Orphan Train who find themselves in a new surrounding, but part of them wishes they had never left the streets. You sort of like the farm, but you miss the hustle and excitement of the big city. For a new Christian who is caught between old values and new, double-mindedness can be extremely disconcerting. You want to act like a Christian, but part of you wants to act like a non-Christian, too. You don't want to completely commit yourself just yet.

It's not a new problem. You can read about people facing it all through the Bible. One couple, Ananias and Sapphira, died be-cause they couldn't handle it.

At that time Roman taxes were causing an economic depression. The Christians got hit harder than anyone else, so they were sharing everything they had. Sometimes in a government class you'll hear this referred to as the first time communism appeared on the earth. Well, these people didn't know communism from rheumatism. They simply didn't think it was a good thing to see other people starve. So they sold their property and used the money to help each other.

This couple, Ananias and Sapphira, decided to sell some land and bring the money to the church to be divided up. That was what a lot of people were doing. But after they sold the land they began to wonder whether it was really a good idea. What if some kind of emergency hit them? So they decided to go halfway. They kept some of the money themselves and brought the rest to church, pretending it was the full amount.

Ananias arrived at church about three hours before his wife. He presented the money to Peter. But Peter knew it wasn't the full amount. "Why are you doing this?" he asked. "You didn't have to. It was strictly voluntary to sell the land in the first place.

by JAY KESLER

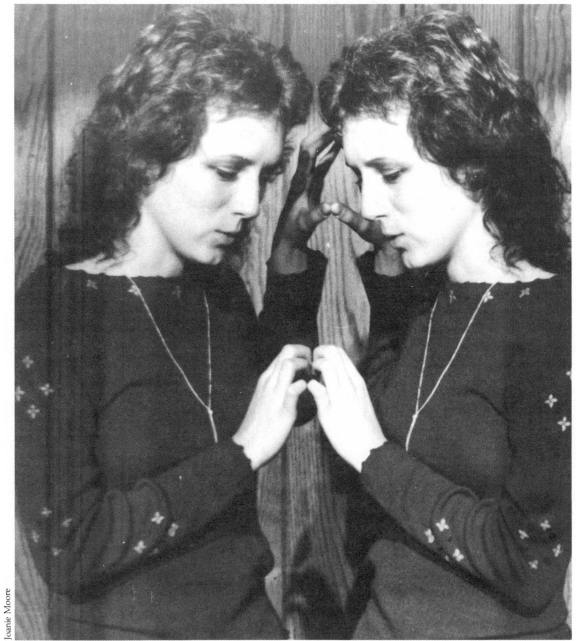

Joanie Moore

And why are you lying that this is all the money you received? You aren't lying to me, you know. You're lying to God himself!" And at those words Ananias fell dead, and they took him out and buried him.

Three hours later Sapphira came in. Peter asked her, "Is this how much you got for the land?" She said, "Yes." Peter said, "Here come the men who just buried your husband for telling the same lie. They'll carry you out, too." And Sapphira fell at his feet and died. The Bible says that "great fear" came on the church.

It's not hard to imagine why. Evidently God doesn't choose to work that way today, but can you imagine what it would be like if he did? Can you hear someone saying, "Man, down at First Methodist, they don't mess around. You tell a fib, and it's all over."

Of course, there's a lot of the story we don't know. We don't know if Ananias and Sapphira were really Christians. We don't know if there were other things they had done. But we can see one thing: they wanted to trust in God, but not trust in him 100 percent. It couldn't be done. They had to choose.

Living Through a Keyhole

Some Christians will try to tell you the world's way of living isn't pleasurable. That's nonsense. If sin weren't pleasurable, there would be no conflict. It isn't sinning that makes you miserable — it's trying to live with your conscience *while* you're sinning. If you could be totally committed to sin as a way of life, you wouldn't have a problem.

Of course, that's the short-term view. In the long run your life would be literally hell. But for right now, sin is fun. It's the Christians who get involved in sin who are miserable.

They've closed the door on sin and then spend their lives looking through the keyhole.

A Christian in this position reminds me of how people in some parts of the world catch monkeys. They drill a hole in a coconut and scrape out all the inside. Then they put in a small piece of candy. When the monkey comes along he sticks his hand into the hole, which is just big enough for his arm, and grabs the sweet. Then he discovers he has a problem. He can't get his fist out of the hole. The only way he can get out is to let go of the candy.

But he's too greedy for that. He'll scream and bang the coconut around, but he won't let go. Eventually a hunter will come along, bop him on the head and put him in a sack. It's safe to assume that the monkey wanted to stay away from the hunter a whole lot more than he wanted the candy. But he wouldn't make the choice. It ended up ruining him.

In humans we call this double-mindedness. The Bible author James says double-minded people are unstable in everything they do. They can't or won't make up their minds, so they're gradually corrupted in everything. Everything! Sometimes people think that only parts of them will become corrupt, maybe their religious life. But it doesn't work that way.

1. Double-mindedness corrupts your relationship with yourself. You can fool other people most of the time, but you can't fool yourself. If you look in the mirror and find yourself as phony as a $3 bill, you lose self-respect. You begin to feel that other people are watching you, even if they're not. You punish yourself.

2. Double-mindedness corrupts your relationship with other people. People see through you more than you think. If you say you're a Christian and then don't act that way, others

will notice it. They won't take you seriously.

I saw an example of this at camp once. A girl was constantly asking that we pray for her friends, her boyfriend, for all kinds of people. She was almost uncomfortably religious. Every time we would ask for some feedback after a talk she'd be the first to respond.

One night during a meeting her boyfriend and some other guys showed up at the camp. They were rough-looking guys, riding motorcycles, and they came into the meeting and sat in the back. At the end we asked those who wanted to commit themselves to Christ to come into a room off the side to talk, and this girl came forward. I wondered at the time, "Why her?" since she seemed like such a super saint. But I had an opportunity to talk to her, along with her boyfriend, who had followed her up to the front.

"I've been a real phony," she said. She told me she and her boyfriend had been involved in this and that together, and how ashamed they were. She was crying, and she looked at him and cried some more and then talked to me some more. Then she said she really wanted to be 100 percent — to give her life entirely to Christ and not be phony any more.

Her boyfriend interrupted and said, "Do you really mean that?" He couldn't believe it.

But she said she really did. "I mean it so much that if you don't want to have anything more to do with me, that's OK. I still want to be a Christian."

So he said to me, "Me, too!" He wanted to give himself to Christ. "I never thought you meant it about being a Christian," he told her. "I thought it was just something you did for your folks, and when we got together it was different. But if it means that much to you there must be something to it. I want to

get a look at it myself." So I spent the next hour or so explaining it to him, and he prayed to accept Christ. Up until then he'd seen only double-mindedness. When he saw genuine, total commitment, he knew there was something very different about it.

3. Double-mindedness corrupts your relationship to God. God is more concerned with a sincere, committed heart than anything else. How we act is important, but it isn't worth a thing if it's just for show. The Bible says that David was a man after God's own heart. But David did everything wrong you can think of. He was an adulterer and a murderer. But he was really committed to God, and God loved him for that despite some tragic mistakes.

You're not fooling God if your commitment to him isn't total. Sometimes we use our relationship to God as a sort of fire escape for emergencies. We don't want God to disconnect the phone, although we'd rather he didn't call us up all the time, either. But the joy of relating to him goes away. Soon there's only a shell we're putting on for other people.

Eternal Toothache

You have to decide between two kinds of pain. One is the pain of total surrender — of saying, "Christ, I really want to do what you want, and nothing is going to stand in my way any longer. You're the most important thing in my life." That is painful sometimes. You may have to give up some things you don't want to give up. But it's like the pain of having a tooth pulled — you dread it and worry about it, but you know sooner or later you have to face it. If you don't face that pain, you get the pain of double-mindedness. It's like a toothache that never stops. It may

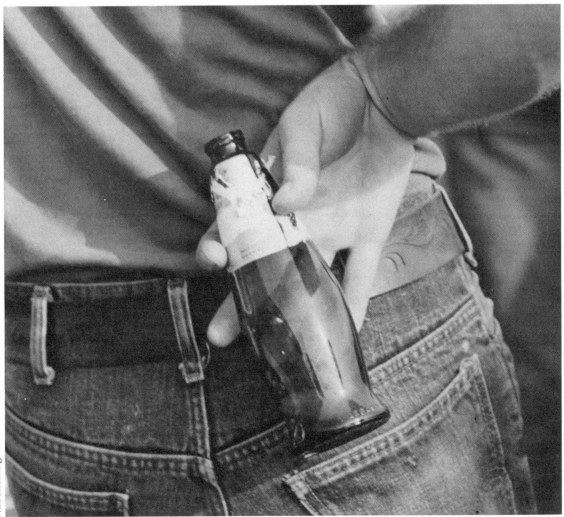

not be as excruciating, but it's a gnawing, agonizing pain. Christians living with this pain can spend their whole lives with a sense of worthlessness, because they won't make the total commitment to Christ that's necessary.

That commitment is different for everyone. There are certain areas, however, which are key ones for students. One is the kind of friends you are going to spend your time with. Some aren't affected by people around them — in fact, they thrive in an adverse environment. They tend to affect the people around them much more than they're affected. But others absorb whatever environment they're in. If you're one of those in the latter category, your complete commitment to Christ may involve cutting off old friendships and finding a new social circle. It will be painful. Don't kid yourself that it won't. But if you're going to lose the pain of double-mindedness, it may have to be done.

Are you going to trust God to give you the ideal sex life inside marriage? Or are you going to mess around?

Another crucial area for some of us is in the habits we can pick up. I'm thinking particularly of drugs and alcohol. Don't pretend to yourself that you're committed to Christ when you're abusing your body. Do you trust Christ to provide what you need, or don't you? If you do, then you don't need crutches.

And are you going to trust God to give you the ideal sex life inside marriage, with the ideal partner of his choice? Or are you going to mess around with the opposite sex trying to provide for yourself? God wants us to be pure sexually, and as a Christian you know it. But are you sufficiently committed to him to act like it?

Maybe you've started thinking about your goals in life. If God wants something from you that will contribute to other people more than just make money for you, are you ready for it? Are you willing to make it your goal, to work and plan for it? Are you going to do the best you can? It isn't easy to work hard at school. But if God wants you to be doing something worthwhile for him in life, it's probably going to be necessary.

There are many other issues. Maybe it's a commitment to pray and study the Bible regularly that you need to make. Wishing it's so isn't enough. Any choice you make for commitment to Christ is going to cost something.

Now, if you give yourself totally to Christ, that doesn't mean that it's done for all time. Total commitment has been defined as giving all you know of yourself to all you know of God. It's only natural that as you learn more about yourself and God, new commitments will have to be made. It will be necessary again and again.

Giving yourself totally to Christ doesn't guarantee that you'll never sin again, either. You won't always do what you want to do. But at least if you've decided for Christ it will be clear-cut. When you blow it, you'll know you blew it. There'll be no doubt. You can ask forgiveness from God and get back on the right track. Your mind will still be set in the right direction. You won't be caught in the middle of two desires.

I'm convinced this is the key to real mental health. Those who really know what they want in life, who are going toward that direction and aren't trying to do two things at once, are going to be pretty stable. Not that they are fanatics — they can be aware of their own failings, and they can have a sense of humor about what they are doing.

But you've made the choice. You have chosen to live for Christ because that's the only thing in life that's worthwhile. You have seen that it means giving up some other very pleasurable things that aren't good for you. And you have given them up. You have given yourself up, totally, to Jesus Christ.

Living On An Island

Changing values not only create internal struggle, they can also cause conflicts with those around you — your friends who aren't Christians. Unlike the war from within, this struggle involves the feelings of others, not only your own. That's what makes it so difficult. To your friends you are not a happy new Christian; you're a once-normal person who has suddenly gone slightly daffy. They hope you'll recover, but if you don't . . . too bad. How do you cope?

Picture this: you are exploring a cave with your friends on a hot and sunny afternoon. It's cool inside the cave so you wander further and further along the winding corridors until you all become hopelessly lost in the darkness. You sit down and try to decide what to do. One of the corridors must lead out, but which one?

Day after day you wander aimlessly in the dark, trying desperately to find the way out. Always you return to the same spot. Just when you think you're lost forever, you spot a light at the end of one of the corridors — it was so easy you don't know how you could have missed it all this time. You race back to

your friends to tell them freedom is at hand — you know the way out. But when you reach them with the news they all act like you're crazy. One says, "Oh, sure, you've found it when no one else has ever been able to." "It's fine for you, but I must try to find my own way out," someone else says. Another voice comments, "Big deal! I like living in the cave; it suits me just fine. Why should I change now?"

So, instead of following you out of the darkness and into the light, they go on grimly living in the cave, as desperate as ever. How does that make you feel?

If you are a Christian and your friends are not, you already know how that feels. You live that imaginary story every day in real life — it's no wonder that new Christians can sometimes feel lonely and frustrated around the very people they thought were their friends. They feel a little like Robinson Crusoe, living on an island all by themselves. What can they do?

Only the Lonely

As a new Christian you may sometimes feel strangely lonely around old friends. This loneliness comes from the fact that communication on many levels is squelched. You don't

by STEVE LAWHEAD

Bob Combs

feel free to share your innermost thoughts and feelings anymore. How can you relate the wonderful closeness you now feel with God to someone who isn't sure there *is* a God?

There is another force at work, too. Now that you are a Christian you have begun meeting other Christians and feel more and more a part of God's family. Your old friends may not understand that it makes sense for you to spend time with your new Christian friends; they can easily misread you here. To them it looks like you have given them up. They think you imagine yourself "too good" for them; parents sometimes feel the same uneasiness. To most everyone who knew you before you were a Christian, it appears that you have abandoned them.

Try to imagine it from their point of view. "Everything was fine until you became a Christian, and then, *bam!* Suddenly old friends aren't good enough anymore — you would rather spend all your time with your new Christian friends. What did we do?" they wonder.

Most likely you will want to continue being friends with people you knew before you became a Christian. And unless they are openly hostile, try to tear down your faith or lead you into places you know Christians shouldn't go, there's no reason to drop them as friends. But because you will be spending more time with new Christian friends you may need to find new ways of sharing with your non-Christian friends. Otherwise, you could find yourself being avoided and left out.

So, if you're feeling a little lonely, remember that your friends and family may be feeling a little lonely, too. If you want support and encouragement, you may have to become very creative in your relationships. After all, you can't expect your friends to support something that is taking you away from them. If anything, they'll try to discourage it to get you back. Being creative in a relationship might mean that you will have to work harder at being a good friend. It might mean that you set aside extra time just to spend with others, or that you go out of your way to initiate activities when before you just tagged along. Maybe you will have to make a special effort to find things you and your friends still have in common that you both can share and enjoy. The point is to keep your faith from becoming a barrier to people who need to see up close what Christians are like.

Life at the Speed of Light

Something happens to you when you become a Christian that makes you want to share what you've got with everyone. You feel positively contagious! Unfortunately, your family and friends may not share your enthusiasm — no matter how hard you try to infect them. Their refusal to have anything to do with your "new religion" can be puzzling and frustrating. *Why can't they see it?* you wonder. *This is the best thing ever! What's wrong with them?* You have all these new feelings and sensations — you feel you'll burst if you can't share them with your friends, tell them why you are changing and how they can change, too.

It's easy to get frustrated in that situation, and the only antidote to frustration is patience. Changes, especially major life changes, take a lot of time. Your friends and family need time to think about what you're telling them. They need time to watch you and to make sure what you say is true, that it's not just another fad — like roller skating — that you're into.

Your friends have a right to a certain amount of skepticism. They know you pretty well — well enough to remember the hobbies that have lasted only a month, the burning romances that fizzled out overnight, the resolutions to "be different from now on," which were forgotten by lunchtime. Your parents have an even longer association with your fickle personality. How do they know this fad won't disappear as soon as a new one appears on the horizon? Christianity may be the best thing in your world today — but what about tomorrow?

Your friends need to see some stability in you before they can wholly accept what has happened. Expecting them to jump on the rocket with you is probably expecting too much. As a new Christian you feel like you are living at the speed of light; everything — all the new things you're learning, the many ways you're growing — is moving so fast. But have enough patience to realize that it is simply too fast for non-Christians to accept. They need more time.

The Squeeze Play

A Christian in a non-Christian environment lives under all kinds of pressure — some of it obvious, and some of it quite subtle. Conformity is the code of high school and college, in a different way. When you go against that code — which, by definition, as Christians, you do — your friends apply pressure to make you quit rocking the boat. Your friends want assurance from you: that gossiping about teachers or other students, forming cliques and carousing on weekends filled with booze and making out, etc. are OK. If you don't agree, or don't support their lifestyle anymore, they have two choices: either bring you back into the fold or blackball you completely.

Again, try to put yourself in your friends' place. What if someone you had known for a long time came up to you one day and told you your life had been a waste, and further-more, the only way to set it right was to do exactly as he said. How would that make you feel? A bit defensive? Hostile?

So go easy on people around you. Forget about using scare tactics. Explosive witnessing and boldly challenging lifestyles may not be your best bet around your friends and loved ones. They are reached better through kind words and a good example. If what you have is worth getting close to, they will see that in you.

Fair Warning

Jesus knew there would be problems in following him; he knew his coming would divide people. "Do you think I have come to give peace to the earth?" he asked his followers one day when they complained about the problems they faced. "From now on families will be split apart, three in favor of me, and two against — or perhaps the other way around. A father will decide one way about me; his son the other; mother and daughter will disagree . . . " (Luke 12:51-53, Living Bible). Jesus accurately foresaw the trouble ahead for his followers.

But that is also your greatest comfort when as a Christian you face loneliness, frustration, and pressure; Jesus knows and understands what you're going through. He, better than anyone else, can help you, comfort you, and prepare you to deal with the problems. Older Christians who have been through the same things you are experiencing now can also help. And, happily, through time, patience, and endurance, God can change things. Remember, though, Jesus can never guarantee that your family or friends will become Christians. That choice is theirs alone to make. If you want them to respect your decision, you must ultimately respect theirs. But one thing you as a Christian can do for your friends that no one else can do is pray for them. Sometimes that's *everything*.

Red Chair Incident

My home had always been like a fireworks factory; one temper would go off and the whole place would explode. Eventually we'd patch up the shattered relationships, but the repairs were only temporary.

I guess I had the shortest fuse in the family. I was always mouthy. And when I got mad, I blasted everyone and everything with bitterly hateful words. Yet deep inside I loved my family, and I could hardly wait to get home from camp to tell them what had happened. I wanted them to share my excitement.

With a suitcase in one hand and a sleeping bag under my other arm, I hurried up the walk in sort of a clumsy jog and burst into the house. "*Guess* what happened to me this week?" I exclaimed. Before anyone had a chance to ask "What?" I grinned and proudly announced, "I became a Christian."

"But you were a Christian before you went to camp," Mom said.

I could see from my sisters' expressions they were thinking the same thing. I tried to explain that being a Christian meant more than going to church. I told about the decision I'd made, the prayer asking Christ to come into my life. But none of my words seemed to penetrate the "Do you believe this?" looks I saw flashing back and forth between my sisters.

I quickly gave up in frustration and stalked off to my room to unpack. *I don't know why I ex-pected anything more from Mom or my sisters,* I thought, blaming their response on their usual inability to understand me. *I should have known.*

Later, I ventured into the empty living room, flicked on the TV, and settled into my favorite chair. It was a huge, overstuffed red chair, big enough for a person to curl up in luxurious comfort. As the prime seat in the house, it was the family favorite for reading and TV.

I had been camped in the chair only a few minutes when my oldest sister, Linda, walked in and flopped down on the floor in front of the tube. During the next commercial I went into the kitchen for a Coke and returned to discover she had pirated the red chair.

I blew up, "You get out of that chair!"

"No," Linda calmly responded without even taking her eyes off the TV screen.

"But I was there first," I insisted. "Get up!"

"No," she responded.

At about that point, Mom came in to see what the shouting was about. When she saw it was only one of our typical chair fights, she told us to cut it out and left. She had hardly left the room before we were at it again in lowered tones. The fight degenerated into insults and name calling about as quickly as the volume rose again to scream level.

We were both fuming when Linda stopped right in the middle of a sentence, shot me a contemptuous look and said calmly, "If you were really a Christian, you'd let me have the chair."

by NANCY DAN as told to GREGG LEWIS

"That has nothing to do with this," I snapped. But her haughty smirk infuriated me and I stormed out of the room.

The next night there was a special Campus Life meeting for all who had become Christians at camp. The club director, Ron Hutchcraft, talked about some problems we would face as new Christians. Then he asked us to share problems we had had.

I recounted the cool reception I had gotten when I returned home and announced my new faith in God. I gave a brief account of the chair fight, building up to the point where I said, "And then she said if I was really a Christian I ought to let her have the chair!"

But instead of sympathizing, Ron looked right at me and said, "I think your sister was right."

Ron's words hit me like a club. For the first time I realized that being a Christian had implications for every area of my life — even with my family. If I wanted my family to listen to what I had to say about being a Christian, my actions would have to match my talk. I determined right then to prove to them that my faith made a difference in my life.

A couple days later I got my first big test. I left the chair for a minute and returned to find Linda in it. I could see she was braced for a scrap and I almost started to yell at her. But I caught myself in time and just sat down on the floor without a word. I didn't look at her, but I could tell she noticed.

Surrendering the chair was tough for a few days. It was a symbol for me. Whenever I felt like I had been cheated out of it, I still felt like fighting. I would have to catch myself and remember that my willingness to surrender my rights and power could be the thing to convince the rest of my family that being a Christian really made a difference in a person's life. And as time passed, the chair didn't seem so important; sometimes I would even get up and offer it to someone else.

I tried to carry my chair attitude over into other areas of life at home. It wasn't easy. The old habits hung on, but praying about it helped. And most of the time when I felt like lashing out at someone in the family, I would stop myself by thinking of the situation as another "red chair incident."

Gradually I sensed a shift of moods at home. As I quit fighting and began to give in, everyone fought less. And as time passed and they realized the change in me wasn't just a temporary thing, people began to listen to what I had to say about my faith.

Two years passed before Linda started to read the Bible to prove that what I was telling her about Christianity was wrong. Instead, the Bible convinced her I was right and she accepted Christ.

But it wasn't until several months after Linda became a Christian that I realized the significance the red chair had had in influencing my family toward Christ. About two years after the first "red chair incident" Linda and I ran into Ron Hutchcraft one evening.

I introduced them and Linda grinned at Ron and asked, "Now that I'm a Christian, Ron, which one of us gets the chair?"

A Detective Story

Growing, changing, forming new values — that's often lonely, frustrating work. But there is a source of comfort available to help ease the loneliness and a guide to help reduce the frustration: it's the Bible.

The Bible is the written record of God's family — people who have faced the same problems and had the same feelings you do now. Sadly, many new Christians overlook this valuable help the Bible can give. To them, the Bible seems like any other musty old history text about some half-remembered clan of eccentrics. But to those who know how to read it, the Bible can be as exciting as a modern detective thriller.

Many people think the Bible is like any other great book. Like *Moby Dick*, for instance; or *David Copperfield*. It is thick, old, has a lot of pages — real thin ones covered with the tiniest print possible. It is a classic, to be sure. But no one is really much interested in reading classics.

For Christians, however, the Bible is like an Owner's Manual for a new life. Once you've read very far into it you'll see that the Bible isn't like a novel (as many vaguely suppose), or any other book you would ever read. It is unique. And by doing a little detective work you'll be able to discover many things you've never considered — how the Bible was written, who wrote it and why, where it came from, and what it means.

To help get you started off on the right trail, here is a crash course for all future Bible detectives.

Who Wrote the Book of Love?

The Bible wasn't written by a single author in the regular sense. It was the work of many hands over an enormous period of time. A collection of writings — history, poetry, wise sayings, drama, songs, theology, and more — the Bible is a book of books, all held together by a single common thread: God.

The Bible is the story of God told in different ways and through various means. In the Old Testament we can trace the actions of God working through his people. Although they were often foolish, inconsistent, and unperceiving, such men were used by God to prepare the way for a better view of himself. In the New Testament we finally see the total picture of God: Jesus. Jesus is the full expression of God as a man. We see him through

by STEVE LAWHEAD

the eyes of his followers and others who knew him, since Jesus himself wrote nothing that has come down to us.

The Bible has been called the Book of Love, and so it is — the story of God's love for his children. It is such an all-encompassing story it takes many different approaches to tell even a part of it. Each writer perceived a slightly different facet of God's multi-faceted nature. But each was guided in his understanding by God himself.

Eventually someone began compiling the letters or books. With the passing away of the early fathers — those closest to Jesus, those who knew him personally, and those who had known the apostles — it became important to have a written record of Jesus' sayings, his teachings and those of the early leaders. The better collections were copied and treasured — so much so that individual copies have come down to us today from that time.

It is important to keep this fact in mind when reading the Bible: the Bible was written first to a specific group of people in a specific part of the world at a specific point in time. Their thoughts, habits, customs — nearly everything about them — were different from our own today.

The Two-thousand Year Filter

Whenever you read the Bible you must be aware that it comes to you through a filter of two thousand years of history. By visualizing the original settings and situations, by traveling back in time to that day and age, you come closer to the true spirit of the Bible.

So, before you ask the question, "How does this passage apply to me?" you must ask, "How did this passage apply to the first readers?" In answering that question you will more surely answer your first question. This additional step cannot be skipped without coloring the meaning, or perhaps vastly altering it.

For example, in 1 Corinthians 11:4-12, the apostle Paul spends some time talking about how a person should pray. He says that men should pray without covering their heads, but that "a woman brings shame on her head if she prays or prophesies bare-headed; it is as bad as if it were shaved." He concludes by saying that "If a woman is not to wear a veil, she might as well have her hair cut off." How do you interpret that? Taking it at face value, you would have no other choice but to force every woman to wear a veil to church next Sunday — or keep the scissors handy.

But by first determining what the passage meant to the original readers we get quite a different result. To the people Paul was addressing (as in Moslem countries today), veils were a necessity of life — a virtuous woman scarcely appeared in public without one. Also, for a woman to attend church without a veil reminded the people of certain pagan cults. Paul, anxious to avoid any misunderstandings, and conscious of the high esteem Christianity reserved for women, opted for a lenient solution: wear a veil. Indeed, in a time when most women were not even allowed to set foot inside temples, Paul was surprisingly open-minded, although it sounds hopelessly archaic to us today.

When beginning to read a passage it is also a good idea to identify the type of passage you are reading. Is it narrative or poetry? A story or a song? Is it theological in nature or is it historical? This can make a big difference in what you get out of a passage. Poetry certainly speaks to our hearts much differently than does history.

D. Michael Hostetler

To read properly you should treat each passage with the respect that is due it. Find out what type of literature it is — letter, poem, historical note, narrative, etc. Then immerse yourself in its element, visualizing the situation of the people who first read it. When you've done that you can begin to see exactly what the Bible is saying to us today.

Of course, this process is greatly helped by a good modern translation. The King James Version is unparalleled for its beauty of expression in the English language. But the very thing that makes it a delight to read often confuses things for us modern readers: its language is archaic. The meanings of many words have changed since the KJV was written. For example, the simple word "let" which today means "to allow," means just the opposite — "prevent" — in King James English.

Also, most of the newer translations make use of older manuscripts and newer scholastic research that can dramatically affect how we interpret certain passages. In ongoing archaeological work the neat twist is that the newer finds are the older manuscripts. As they peel away the layers of time, pushing further back, archaeologists uncover newer and better information useful to our understanding of the Bible and the people who wrote it. The Dead Sea Scrolls, for example, made a great impact on our understanding of the Old Testament, introducing many new facts of which the KJV writers had no knowledge.

This Book Reads You!

At this point a person might wonder, *if it's this involved, why read the Bible at all?* A fair question. The only answer that means anything in the final analysis is the answer that means something to you. Some people read because the Bible helps direct their lives, and they know they can count on its guidance. Others read it for the comfort and assurance it provides. And some because it challenges them to a higher life. Most, however, read it because in some way they hear the voice of God speaking through it.

Whatever the reason, the Bible is not a book like any other. No one who reads it diligently and thoughtfully comes away the same. The Bible engages you; it changes you. Christians welcome this interaction because, more than being the sourcebook of our faith, it teaches and forms the Christian character as it does so. New Christians are encouraged to read the Bible because of this forming process; the Bible handily equips a person to live the life God requires.

Thus the Bible can be read on many levels. The Bible is able to take you from where you are and lead you on to a different place. There's just one catch: you have to read it. And the key to getting the most out of your reading is preparation — getting yourself ready. To try tackling a lengthy passage on the history of the tribes of Israel late at night, half asleep, with the TV droning on in the background, is not giving the Bible a fair chance. Instead, read it when you are able to give it your full attention, when you are alert and listening for what God has to say to you as you read. The better prepared you are, the more enriched you'll be by your time with God's Word.

Don't be afraid of the Bible. It isn't too sacred or delicate to be put to the test. In fact, it is much more interesting and rewarding when you come to the Bible like a detective searching out clues to the truth. Have your sharpest questions ready, discard all preconceived notions and biases, and just follow wherever the truth leads. You don't have to be afraid of what you will find — although you may be startled out of some of your early ideas about God. Most people are surprised to find that what others say about the Bible is quite different from what the Bible says for itself.

Over the centuries the Bible has become hopelessly entangled in fire-and-brimstone evangelism and holier-than-thou piety, with old-fashioned superstition and crippling literalism, with myth and murky commentary, boring sermons and hysterical ranting. It has been used to justify wars and rationalize injustice of all types.

And yet, in spite of all that, or maybe because of it, the Bible is a book about life the way it really is. It is a book about people who at one and the same time can be both believing and unbelieving, innocent and guilty, saints and sinners, full of hope and full of despair. In other words, it is a book about you. To read it is to come face to face with yourself, and with God.

Something To Think About

We were on our way to Anthropology 378 when Dave said, very casually, "How about coming to Bible Study with me at noon?"

"To what?" I asked, frankly incredulous.

"Bible Study," he repeated, dead serious.

"Bible Study," I hooted. "Why study *that?*"

He didn't answer, really. "About six of us guys have been meeting in Cameron, Room 395," he said. Then he added, "If you came once or twice, you might see why we study it."

"It's just not my line, Dave," I said. But I didn't want to offend him, because Dave is a good guy. So I thought I'd better keep the conversation going for a minute or two longer — to make things sound not quite so rude and abrupt. "You know, Dave," I said, and I was puffing a bit between phrases because I found it hard to keep up with a six-footer's strides and talk too, "I don't really think . . . *(deep breath)* that an intellectually honest person can take the Bible seriously any more."

Intellectual honesty is a great old court of appeal. Dave didn't say anything, so I gasped on.

"Let's face it, everyone knows about the contradictions. . . . " I was doing some fast thinking: it would be like Dave to ask for an example. " . . . and the myths like Adam and Eve and Noah and the boys." I paused to get my breath and get back in step with Dave. "I just don't see that it's honest to go on taking an outmoded book so seriously. That's all."

Dave still didn't say anything. We were almost to class. I thought probably I'd given him something to think about. Maybe neither of us would go to Bible Study at noon today, I thought. We could have lunch together at the cafeteria and go over our anthro notes.

When Dave did say something, he said it so casually I thought he was changing the subject. "Say, Ron," he said. "Speaking of intellectual honesty. . . . "

I fell for it hard. "Yeah?" I said, really interested.

"What do you think of a guy doing a critical review of a book he hasn't read?"

Give me a break!

As told to MAXINE HANCOCK

Eyes That See

Your values affect the way you see things — even ordinary things take on new significance. That's because you begin to see your surroundings a little like God sees them.

Without God	Goofing off is great. Pure fun . . . maybe. If the right people are there. You wouldn't want to be seen with a bunch of losers — it wouldn't look good.
With God	No person is a loser to God. He made each one and cares deeply about all. Goofing off, or shopping, or studying — every encounter with another person is a chance to be with a person God cares about.
Without God	A glimpse of color against a clear blue sky. A darting in the air. A wing in motion. Flight. You watch a bird defy gravity and it tugs at your heart to follow. Your soul responds. To what? It's only a bird. A mass of bones and feathers that evolution has taught a few tricks. That's all.
With God	The same bird. The same thrill at the sight. Your heart tugs and you breathe thanks to God for his beautiful creatures. He loved the world enough to make it beautiful. That's the kind of God he is. Nature is no accident. Everything God does carries his signature, so you begin to see God in everything.
Without God	There's a pleasure in making something out of nothing. A lump of clay becomes a pitcher. Earth becomes a handsome utensil. But why? For the money it'll bring? For recognition as a craftsman? For your own artistic expression?
With God	You realize your artistic drive comes from God the Creator. The joy you feel in your creation is his joy, too. You realize that God made the universe with as much care as you lavish on your hunk of clay. You are linked to God — a mini-creator. With God you are an artist who makes things as much for the joy of creation, as for the joy of sharing that creation with someone else.

Bob Combs

Without God

This part of town is something to avoid.
It's a curse. An eyesore. Why don't these people do
something about it?
They're so lazy — that's why they're poor.
You feel vaguely guilty, but it's not your fault.
What can one person do, anyway?

With God

Poverty and suffering are not part of God's plan.
They are symptoms of a disease the human race
has contracted. A disease that, without God,
is terminal.
Death results. Not instantly, not painlessly. But
slowly and surely.
The street is a reminder: all is not fun with friends,
the joy of birds in flight, pleasure in making
pottery.
Life is more than pleasure and possessions.
There is serious work to be done.
Without God, someone could die.
With God, someone can live.

The Family Treasure

Suppose you were born into the ruling family of England. You would be as helpless as any other newborn baby. But you would grow up knowing that someday you would have a share of the family wealth, and the throne. Wouldn't that make a substantial difference in the way you lived every day?

You would quickly get used to being called Prince or Princess. State dinners and royal outings would become commonplace; the finest treasures would be yours for the asking.

Something even more remarkable happens when you become a Christian. You are instantly adopted into the family of God. You become an heir to the wealth of the Universe-maker. The treasures of a billion stars are yours, all the wealth of galaxies yet undiscovered belong to him, and are yours as a member of his family. That doesn't mean that you can immediately move into a palace or buy yourself a Lear jet by charging it to your heavenly account. God has something different in mind for his heirs — vastly different than bulging billfolds, Swiss bank accounts, or any other measure of worldly wealth.

Life in heaven is going to be fulfilling, satisfying — a life of peace and purpose, joy and happiness. Endlessly. Forever. That's incomprehensible. But that's the promise God makes to his heirs. Yet, the promise of God's inheritance means more than a future dream. It also calls us to a purpose-filled life here, right now. When you were born into your family you didn't have to wash the car or clean out the basement before your name was typed on the birth certificate. But as you grow older, becoming an active, contributing member of the family does mean accepting some responsibility. You are expected to help out, to contribute your share toward the work of sustaining the family.

This section explores the various responsibilities that come to us as members of God's family. Just as your natural family is the place where you learn about yourself in relation to others, so in God's family you grow to become more attuned to the feelings of those around you. And, perhaps just as importantly, you are to reach out to those outside the Christian family, to welcome others into the family. Part of being an heir to an eternal and inexhaustible family fortune means that you try to get as many people as possible to share it with you.

Drastic Action

One of the responsibilities God gives the members of his family is to love others. Christians believe love supplies the answers to life's tough questions — maybe not easy answers, but ones that make sense. However, the kind of love that answers hard questions is not a passive word. It has no real meaning until translated into action.

Ask a group of Christians what they consider to be the "Number 1" responsibility of the Christian. 50 percent will probably say "sharing Christ with others"; 30 percent will most likely answer "worshiping and serving God"; about 10 percent will say "prayer"; and the remaining 10 percent will volunteer "Bible study."

Those are all good things to keep in mind, but none are anywhere close to the most important responsibility.

Surprised? Most people are. Well, then, what is it that God considers a Christian's Number 1 responsibility? A group of very religious people asked Jesus that same question. They asked him, "Teacher, which is the greatest commandment in the law?" He an-swered with not one, but two that he considered equally important. Jesus replied, "Love God with all your heart, mind and soul. This is the first and greatest commandment. And the second is like it: Love your neighbor as you love yourself." Jesus then indicated that everything else was secondary to these two commandments that he viewed as one. (Matthew 22:34-40.)

Loving others is the most important responsibility of those who want to follow Jesus. Prayer and Bible study are important for growth as a Christian; and going to church every Sunday is good, too. Why weren't one of those given as the answer?

Maybe because those things, like most things people do every day, are personally directed — that is, they are intended for you. They help you, but may not mean much to others. Time and again the Bible challenges its readers to take drastic measures in the pursuit of loving others. This "drastic love" does not originate from the same place, nor is it expressed in the same way as other kinds of love.

Think about it. When you fall in love with another person, what do you feel like? How do you act? You might think about him or her during the day, dreaming up things you'll

by STEVE LAWHEAD

say, or planning special times together. You feel warm when you think of that person; there's no one else you'd rather be with.

There are other kinds of love, too, of course. The love you have for your country is a feeling of pride, a stirring in your heart when the flag goes by. Then there's the love you have for your friends: that certain spark you feel when you're with them that makes you wish time would stand still so you could just enjoy each other.

There's a common thread running through all those different kinds of love: the feeling you get. All of them depend on the emotion that plays within you. That emotional charge is how you know you are experiencing love.

The Radical Difference

But the kind of love Jesus had in mind was completely different. It's origin was not rooted in the emotions, and its expression does not depend on enjoying the other person or even the presence of the other person. This "drastic love" Jesus lived was action-oriented. It originates in action and is expressed in action. It is not something you *feel*; this love is something you *do*.

This difference is a big one, quite radical when you think about it. But also totally reasonable. Jesus no doubt knew that human beings can no more control their emotions than they can control the monsoon season in Tibet. So he simply bypassed emotions altogether when he commanded this kind of love. The fact that he commanded it at all should be a clue — you can't *command* an *emotion*, but you can command an *action*. He didn't say, "*Try* to love your neighbor." He said, "Do it!"

Jesus lifted this love out of the realm of the emotions and placed it in the arena of the will. He made it possible for us to *choose* to love this way. This has an interesting effect: when love is expressed as an action — a good deed, a kind word, a helping hand — it is possible to love people we don't even particularly like. Why is this possible? For the

The kind of love Jesus was talking about isn't a warm, gushy feeling somewhere in the pit of your stomach.

simple reason that it doesn't matter one ion how you feel about an action as long as you do it.

When a five-star General tells an enlisted man to shine his boots, he's not greatly concerned how the private feels about shining boots. The main thing is that the man's boots appear with a glossy sheen the next time the General sees him.

Of course, it would probably be better for all concerned if soldiers really liked shining boots. But perhaps a strange and wonderful transformation would occur if enlisted men saw how good shined boots looked, how pleased the General was to see them shined and how good it felt to walk around in spotless, snappy boots — they would begin to actually feel good about shining them. Maybe they would even begin to shine their boots spontaneously, without being ordered to.

The love that Jesus commands cuts far deeper than shining boots, but his command carries no less weight than the supreme commander of the armed forces. It is to be obeyed by all who follow him — gladly, if possible, but followed in any case.

Many people are not used to taking orders. It's doubly difficult when following the order seems to go against all common sense. But maybe the answer here is practice. Once you get used to the idea that loving is doing, you begin to find all sorts of ways to express your love for your neighbor: cleaning the gutters for the widow down the street; delivering brownies to a sick friend; giving outgrown clothes to Goodwill; helping the family next door pack for moving day; inviting guests for dinner. . . . The more you begin to do, the more you'll find to do.

Again, Jesus has not left us on our own; he doesn't demand that we do anything he himself doesn't do. He left us a blueprint, a pattern for carrying out his command: his own example.

As Christians we are commanded to take this "drastic action" way of loving others. And when you follow through you'll become aware of a unique phenomenon: the ripple effect. You see it when you throw a rock into a pond — ripples spreading out in concentric rings from a single source. If you throw a big enough rock into the pond, the ripples become waves by the time they reach the shore. It's an unavoidable law of nature; a million rocks thrown into a million ponds produce exactly the same result each and every time.

Jesus Loves the Unlovely.

Time and time again Jesus made an effort to go beyond his intimate circle of friends to reach people whom most would have considered unreachable. He loved the poor, he loved his enemies, he loved people who were not very lovable.

This should be a model for us. Too often we're drawn only to those who are attractive and popular. We find it easy to care for the "nice" people. What about those who are not so nice? We tend to ignore them: the quiet guy with braces who always sits in the back of the room; the girl with acne so bad she can't hold her head up; the short, mouthy kid who's always popping off with a smart remark. . . . We don't often notice them for what they are — people who need love.

Most of us would be content to spend our lives caring only about the people closest to us, our family and friends. But Jesus reminds us that this isn't really worth much on his scale of values. "If you love only those who love you, what good is that? Even scoundrels do that much. If you are friendly only to your friends, how are you different from anyone else? Even heathens do that" (Matthew 5:46-47, Living Bible).

Clearly he expects us to go beyond our own inclinations, to seek out more difficult assignments in love.

This isn't easy. But the kind of love Jesus was talking about isn't a warm, gushy feeling somewhere in the pit of your stomach. In fact, the kind of love Jesus demands has little to do with feelings at all (or at least not the kind we usually think of).

Jesus' Love Is Tough.

Jesus' idea of love would make nearly every one of us uncomfortable: it means sweat, sacrifice, and stamina. He told us that caring for another person could prove costly. "If someone slaps you on one cheek, let him slap the other too! If someone demands your coat, give him your shirt besides. Give what you have to anyone who asks you for it; and when things are taken away from you don't worry about getting them back" (Luke

108

6:29-30, Living Bible).

Jesus' kind of caring is something you do, not something you feel. Jesus displayed that in the ultimate way — his own death. For love he sacrificed his life; because he cared about us he allowed himself to be put to

If you wait for a rush of soupy emotions you will probably miss out.

death. I doubt if warm, fuzzy feelings would have motivated Jesus to give himself to be nailed to a cross in agony. He did what had to be done regardless of how he felt.

Often we make the mistake of thinking we have to develop some kind of "inner glow" or mushy feeling toward others before we can do anything for them. We think that we have to *feel* love for others to *want* to do good things for them. If we felt warm toward that crotchety old man, we would visit with him or take him shopping. However, the kind of tough love Jesus demands short circuits that idea. He tells us to love others by *doing*, by helping them. When you see someone who needs your care, do what you know you should. If that makes you feel good inside, fine. But don't count on good feelings to motivate. Chances are if you wait to be motivated by a rush of soupy emotions you will miss most of the opportunities you have to love and care for others.

Jesus' Love Is Generous.

When you look at Jesus walking among the people you see him giving to anyone who asks for help. Tax collectors, Roman soldiers, beggars, prostitutes, thieves, etc. — all felt free to come to him because he put no price tags on his love. Jesus loved freely. He loved the good and the bad alike without making distinctions.

Jesus never paused to ask himself, "If I loved so-and-so, what would people think of me?" or "If I healed this person, what's in it for me?" His love and kindness were selfless. You might even say that he was reckless with his love, giving it away with both hands. He never held back — even when it hurt. When someone came to Jesus with a problem, Jesus became totally involved with that person, and there were no strings attached. However, there was *one* thing he required of the people who came in contact with his love: they were to go and do likewise.

Jesus' kind of love leaves little room for superficial emotional displays; it's much deeper than a sappy greeting of the hearts and flowers variety. Real love means going out and caring for those who need friends: the awkward, the shy, the hostile, the dull, the slow, the odd — those who don't seem to be worth much by common standards. That caring has to be demonstrated by real work — giving your time, energy, and resources to those who need them, no thought for yourself and no strings attached. That is an almost impossible order, but it is an order nonetheless.

Any time you perform an action of love for another person, you start something that grows beyond the act itself and cannot be contained. If enough Christians took Christ's action love seriously, think what the effect would be — a tidal wave would wash over the whole world. What would that be like? There is a way to find out. Start making a few waves.

Beggar To Beggar

Many things are contagious: mumps, measles, chicken pox. And other things like school spirit on a brisk autumn day, or the thrill of pride as a lively marching band steps out to the "Stars and Stripes Forever." If you are in a crowd of people, and if it's contagious — whatever it is, you'll catch it.

Christianity is contagious. It is spread by human contact, from person to person, one person at a time. Yet, the way some Christians act, you would think they carried the Black Plague and lived in mortal fear of infecting anyone. Of course, that is the opposite of what our attitude should be. But it's hard to overcome that inertia that makes it difficult to tell others about our faith. Karl Barth, noted theologian, boiled years of wisdom down to this: "Christianity is merely one beggar telling another beggar where to find bread." It's that simple, that basic. And that profound.

The question caught Barry completely off-guard. "You're a Christian, aren't you?" Mike had asked. "Why do Christians believe they're right and everyone else is wrong?" While Mike waited for an answer, a knot formed in Barry's throat. He quickly looked around to see if anyone in the quiet study hall was watching him. He wished he could just melt away, disappear.

"What's so special about Christians anyway?" Mike wanted to know. Barry fumbled with his pencil and opened his mouth just as the bell rang. "Uh, I don't know, Mike," he said, shoving back his chair as he scooped up his books. "I gotta go."

Mike shrugged and walked away. Barry felt relieved at first. But on his way to the next class he felt more like kicking himself. He had sat behind Mike in study hall all year. They had shared a lot of things — until today. Barry knew that Christians were supposed to tell others about their faith. But he just plain chickened out.

A Turn-off

Witnessing. The word itself is a turn-off. If you're a Christian reading this chapter, you're probably ready to turn to something else. If you're not a Christian and you've had an awkward experience with someone who has pressured you about God, you may be thinking, "Oh, no! Not an article to encourage more of that!"

by STEVE LAWHEAD

Why does the word "witnessing" strike fear and dread into the hearts of potential witnessers and witness-ees alike? Perhaps it's because people have some wrong ideas about witnessing.

A carnival barker is someone who stands outside a circus tent and cajoles people into seeing the show. Barkers do this by raving about the exotic sights, the thrills, chills and excitement inside. "Step right up! See sights unimagined, the wonders of five continents! Hurry! Hurry! The show is about to begin!"

This is one wrong picture many have about witnessing: Christians standing outside their tents, trying to talk other people inside. But witnessing is more than a practiced speech and smooth style. In fact, it is not merely something you say. If you're a Christian, it's something you *are*. You can't escape being a witness. Through your behavior and lifestyle you display what you believe — even if you never say a word to anyone about Christ.

Yet there are times when witnessing by your lifestyle alone isn't enough — you must loosen up your vocal chords. If you are being a good witness with your life, people will be drawn to you. They'll want to know what makes you different. They'll ask questions. And they may even have some problems and look to you for help.

Another wrong idea about witnessing has to do with the language used to communicate. For some reason, many Christians who talk normally the rest of the time suddenly speak "Christianese" when they talk about their faith. They tell non-Christians it's necessary to "repent," to "accept salvation" and to be "born again." Perhaps they think it sounds more spiritual. But to a person unfamiliar with this kind of language, it just sounds confusing.

Without religious jargon, how do you get through to someone who is outside the Christian faith?

You'll find a list of practical hints following at the end of this chapter. But the basic strategy for communicating with non-Christians can be summed up with one piece of advice: start where that person is. Find some common ground: basic human needs, problems we all share. Then, in your own words, tell how your faith in Christ affects these areas of life. It may take some practice before you feel comfortable sharing with others. But the secret is to be yourself, to be genuine.

Some Christians think they must be perfect before they can witness. But none of us is perfect, and we shouldn't pretend we are. Christians are people with problems and shortcomings — people who sin. And that's important to admit when sharing your faith. After all, no one is interested in listening to a speech from a "saint" with a "holier than thou" attitude. It is our humanness as much as it is our saintliness that appeals to people. When we appear as we really are — former refugees who have found a place of safety and rest — our words have immediacy and impact. We are not "tour guides of God's kingdom," but fellow travelers who have found the right path. We are beggars who must tell other beggars where to find bread.

Some Christians seem to think witnessing is a one-shot, once-and-for-all opportunity. But that's another wrong idea.

Witnesses should care enough about what they have to share, and enough about the person they want to share it with that they'll give their time, energy, and resources to win those persons over. And if, after all they've said and done, their friends still don't become Christians — they shouldn't think they have

Kay Freeman

113

failed.

God wants Christians to participate with him by sharing about him. Jesus made that very clear when he said in Mark 16:15 — "Go into all the world and preach the good news to everyone, everywhere." But if we use the opportunities we have, God is responsible for bringing people to himself. That final step is his responsibility, not ours.

Twelve Hints

There are a few practical things you should keep in mind whenever you set out to tell someone about your faith. Remember to:

1) Be yourself. Being a witness doesn't mean making yourself over into a slick, smiling, self-confident person you're really not. Shyness can be used to witness: some people will never be reached by a person who bowls them over. Humor can be used, and so can deep thinking. The point is to be yourself authentically — not an imitation of something or someone you've seen.

2) Take initiative. We often assume no one is interested in our faith, that if we bring up the subject of Jesus they'll think we're weird. The truth is that opportunities come up most every day. We just have to be alert to them, then dive in. The response is often surprisingly positive.

3) Tell people what you feel. If you're afraid someone will think you're a religious fanatic, say so. "You know, I'm afraid you'll think I'm a religious fanatic for saying this, but I think it's really important. . . . " When people know how you feel, they're more willing to listen.

4) Make friends with people. The people you can best be a witness to are the ones who know you best, and who see you in all kinds of situations, living the life Christ has given you. If you don't have any non-Christian friends, it's time to reevaluate your life. Are you living in a small box?

5) Talk about what people are interested in. Listen to what people have to say. If your friend likes movies, talk about movies, and get into what they really mean. Maybe watching a TV show together will provide a great opportunity to say some things about what life really means, and get into a discussion. If your friend likes sports, talk about sports. There are no end of topics to start discussions — God is Lord of *every* aspect of life.

6) Make sure you know the basics of Christianity. "The Four Spiritual Laws" or something like them can help, because they give you a basic outline you can use with freedom. It keeps you on the subject, especially when you're nervous or unused to talking freely about your faith.

7) Pray sincerely. Being a witness begins in faith, operates in faith, ends in faith. "Witnessing," when it's done outside of trusting God, is simply wrong. You're better off eating a peanut butter sandwich, if that's what God wants you to do. Relax! Let God lead you to opportunities: don't go crazy trying to create them for yourself.

8) Make sure your love doesn't depend on your "victim's" response. If you're all smiles when you talk about God, but you never care about that person once you're convinced he or she won't become a Christian, you're phony. God knows it, and non-Christians know it.

9) Don't be afraid to ask someone to pray with you. If you sense that the person to whom you are witnessing is close to accepting Christ, it's a simple, normal question. Unfortunately, it can be hard to ask: sudden-

ly you get shy.

10) Make sure the person you are talking to understands what he or she is getting into. Jesus Christ is Lord as well as Savior. Emphasize the fact that becoming a Christian means obeying him. A Christian's life isn't *always* happy.

11) Plant truth like seeds. Don't make witnessing something you do at a specific time and place only: mention God in your everyday conversation. When you're going to a meeting of Christians, say so. Don't be afraid to explain what it is. If you've been praying, don't be afraid to mention it. If you've learned something from the Bible, ditto.

12) Don't be weird. Don't ram truth down people's throats, and avoid giving the impression that becoming a Christian means suddenly turning into a Jesus freak, angel, or Bible-thumping evangelist. You don't have to talk about Christ all the time: live Christ.

Many people have a long way to go before they can accept Christ. They're like people standing in a well with one foot on a ladder to climb out. Others may be halfway up the ladder and some may be only one rung from the top. Our witnessing may have helped to move them up a few rungs, although we might not sense much change at first. We might only notice the difference when the person finally steps up out of the well and joins us.

The apostle Paul put it like this: when we share our faith, it's like working together to put in a garden. One person plants the seed, another waters it, and a third reaps the harvest. All three are important, and none of the steps can be skipped.

That Crazy Kid

Richard Wurmbrand, a Protestant minister who spent fourteen years in a communist prison in Rumania, tells this story. He once asked a boy if he believed in the divinity of Christ. The boy answered no.

"If Jesus is God," the boy said, "He should be able to do the things that God does. God made roses and roses make other roses. God made elephants and elephants make other elephants. If Jesus is God, he should be able to make other Jesuses.

"But I have never seen one. My mother takes in washing and has no time for me. My father is an alcoholic. Nobody was ever kind to me, so I never met Jesus."

Wurmbrand then asked the boy, "But isn't your pastor another Jesus?"

"No!" came the emphatic reply.

When Wurmbrand later told the pastor what the boy had said, the pastor answered, "That crazy kid."

You Gotta Be There

Family reunions are the best of times and the worst of times. There are the inevitable height measurements and nose comparisons, the same tired-out old stories dragged from the mothballs and retold for the jillionth time. Peevish Aunt Martha nags boisterous Uncle Fred; babies cry, dogs bark, kids eat too much and get sick, old folks nap in the shade. There's nothing quite like it. But for all the clamor and bother something good takes place. A sense of unity is created that spans generations; family ties are formed and strengthened.

Christians have family reunions, too. Every week. The Sunday service performed in churches the world over can be thought of as a family reunion. It is where Christians come together to share the experience of worship, to encourage one another and to enjoy each other. In belonging to a church, each Christian participates in an ongoing concern that bridges the years.

Ruth Senter discovered that she had developed some wrong ideas about going to church. In setting out to change those ideas she found she was in for a surprise.

by RUTH SENTER

Who needs to go to a football stadium packed full of fanatics, sit on hard, backless bleachers for two or three hours, and eat cold hot dogs to watch a game you can't even see from spectator perches somewhere up in the stratosphere? Why put up with that when you can sit at home in the comfort of your reclining Lazy-Boy, munch potato chips with no interference from the fanatics, and enjoy a bird's-eye view on your TV?"

I dumped that line of logic on my friends the day they returned from the Rose Bowl. They talked about California's giant bowl as though they had just seen one of the Seven Wonders of the World. My skepticism fueled their enthusiasm. "You gotta be there to understand what it's all about," one of my die-hard friends replied.

A couple of years later I went to the Rose Bowl, sat for two-and-a-half hours on hard, backless bleachers, ate cold hot dogs, got my ribs bashed in by an over-zealous Washington fan, came home and told my friends, "You just *have* to be there to know what I mean."

Jim Whitmer

No one has to pack up and go to Pasadena, California, to watch the Rose Bowl. You can see it wherever there's a TV screen. But being there in person adds dimensions to the game that no color TV or Lazy-Boy recliner can begin to offer.

For example, there's the spirit of the game: the electricity that rides the air; the thunder of the crowd ecstatic over a completed pass; the brotherhood of football fans — a common denominator that unites 100,000 people for a short time; the feeling that I'm a part of something that is much bigger than I and my little world; the pull toward involvement when all the fans around you are on their feet telling the players how to run the fourth down on their own ten-yard line. It's a spirit that's hard to capture when you are sitting alone in front of a TV screen.

Being There

My uninformed attitude toward big-time football was much like my former feelings about going to church. "Who needs a church to worship God?" I asked myself. "I can think respectful thoughts about God under the pine trees just as well as under a cathedral ceiling. I can sing songs about God's love in the shower as well as in a choir loft. I can read Psalm 23 in bed as well as standing at attention in a three-piece suit. If worship is a private matter between me and God, why all the public pageantry to promote reverential meditations about him? A person doesn't need stained glass windows, padded pews, and organ chimes to worship God. Why bother, when going to church doesn't make you a Christian any more than swimming in the ocean makes you a fish?"

That's how I felt for a long time. But recently I've come to some conclusions about

worshiping God at church. One is that part of the inspiration to worship comes from others — it's the spirit that a group of people bring to the experience. It seems to me that worship, like football at its best, is a group event — a feeling of love and respect for God that you share with other people. Worshiping God by yourself is a little like going into a fancy restaurant, ordering a steak dinner, and eating it alone: you miss the fun of sharing something good with someone else.

I need the church to help me worship just as I need that same pull toward involvement that comes when I'm in the stadium with the fans. I need to give myself the opportunity to allow a little bit of other people's enthusiasm, hurts, cares, concerns, and interests to rub off on me. I need the spirit of worship that is sometimes hard to capture when I'm sitting by myself at home.

"Think about how you can encourage one another to love and good deeds, and don't forget to come together," a New Testament author wrote to a group of young Christians. The church at its best is a group, sharing in a common experience and inspiring one another to a greater enthusiasm for God.

Sadly, worship of God has been too much like my football-watching habits in other ways too. For years I've half-heartedly followed bowl games. I could probably tell you who played and maybe even the final score. But it's different with Rose Bowl '78. I can tell you anything you want to know about the outstanding runs, kicks, and passes of the game because I was there and the game had my undivided attention.

I didn't spend the usual half of the game running out to the refrigerator for Cokes, refilling the potato chip dish, letting the cat out the back door, answering the phone, turning up the thermostat, or popping a pizza into the oven. I sat and watched football and learned a lot about the Washington and Michigan football teams. The stadium isolated me from distractions and I kept my mind on the game.

The church does the same thing for me when I worship there. I can and have worshiped God under the pine trees along the shores of Lake Michigan. I start out thinking lofty thoughts about the bigness of a God who could make such beauty . . . until a chipmunk starts playing in front of me, or the mosquitoes start to bite, or a sailboat goes by, or I see a butterfly, or smell bacon frying in the campsite just over the hill. Suddenly my thoughts of God are bombarded by a million distractions and my worship washes out with the waves.

True, if I'm looking for excuses to keep me from thinking about God and what he might want to say to me, I can find enough in a church sanctuary to keep me tuned out for an hour or more. But I'm less likely to get up and start doing something else when I'm in the middle of a crowded church pew than if I were sitting by the lake or curled up on my bed at home. I find it much easier to keep my mind on God when I know there's a good possibility that the people around me are thinking about him too, and when I'm in a place that I've come to associate with the worship of God.

A Smorgasbord

The Rose Bowl offered me another dimension that worship in church offers me as well: people. The game is the people: a colorful panorama of uniforms, different teams, positions, bands, loyalties. It is an unlikely blend of spectators: the slick sportscasters, the classy coeds, the windy motorcycle crew that breezed in from Vancouver, the pot-bellied beer drinkers, the silver-haired grandmothers with the seat cushions and plaid football blankets, the casual crowd from the coast, and the conservatives from the Midwest. We were all there, mixed together in that giant bowl. The only difference that anyone even thought about was which team you were pulling for, and even that didn't keep you from feeling like friends, because you all liked football.

The church is people too — a melting pot of personalities, ideas, backgrounds, customs, procedures: the little old lady who thinks rock music will rot your soul; the sexy dancer who used to own the local disco joint; the deacon who never smiles and always wears black suits; the clique of junior high girls who wear tight jeans and never stop laughing; the mother of five who spends her days in PTA, and the striking young female executive who jets around the world.

Who says Christians all need to be the same? Where did we get the idea that people in church need to be exact replicas of one another? We didn't get it from Scripture because the Bible talks about variety; about the church being like different parts of a body — eye, ear, hand, foot. All parts are different, and all are necessary. Going to church reminds me that I need a smorgasbord of people to give balance to my life.

Who needs to go to church? I do. I need to be there in order to see that God's work is much bigger than just what he's doing for me; so I can close out the distractions that keep me from God; so I can learn about being a part of a group and about variety. And I guess when all is said and done, church is like the Rose Bowl my friends tried to tell me about. You have to be there to understand what it's really all about.

Giving Back

There are perhaps as many different ways of serving God as there are people to serve him. If you are serious about following God's will, he is serious about showing you his plan for your life. All you need to do is ask him, and demonstrate a willingness to act on his leading — he won't be slow in showing you what he has in mind. He has a purpose for you and a job that needs doing that only you can do. What is it?

No one likes the idea of pain. We all spend our lives trying to avoid it in all its various disguises: hunger, physical strain, loneliness, unhappiness. No one would consciously choose any of those things if there was a better alternative. Yet Jesus said that those who followed him could expect to encounter pain in their lives; he told everyone to "count the cost" before joining him.

If you seriously want to be a Christian it will cost you something. That's a fact that many preachers and evangelists seem to overlook — they hide the price tag. But realistically, Christianity is not all fun and games; it's not a "happy time" religion, no matter what anyone says. Because, if you're doing it right, you'll run into some painful situations. Jesus calls his followers to account for their material possessions; to be glad when they are persecuted; to abandon all to his leading and his will; to forfeit family, friends, security, and even life itself if he asks.

The cost is different for each person. Just because someone you know says that God wants him to do something doesn't necessarily mean that God wants you to do the same thing. He gave us all different gifts and abilities so that we might serve him in different ways. But God does want you to do *something*; he has very particular plans for you. To find out about those plans means opening your heart and mind to him, seeking his leading above all else.

It's hard to follow the will of God. It can be uncomfortable, even downright painful. A fair number of Christians have died trying. That's part of the cost of being a Christian.

And it is not as if the cost buys you anything — you aren't working your way to heaven. God's love and promises have no price tag. Choosing to follow his will for your life is more like saying "Thank you" for all that he has already given you.

There are several areas that Christians

by TIM STAFFORD

have consistently found appropriate for saying "Thank you" to God. Undoubtedly there are others. But these are good places to start learning where and how God is leading you to start giving back.

Your Home

Who says American Christians should remain comfortable suburbanites? Of course, as long as you're living with your parents you don't have much choice about where you live. But you can begin to think about the future. You can even spend a summer experiencing a different place and lifestyle.

One possibility is the inner city. It's falling apart, and the people stuck in the ruins need help. In most of the major American cities there are groups of Christians who have gotten together to fight the spiritual and physical deterioration. Some of them cluster around a church, setting up programs to help the neighborhood. Some of them live in community, sharing what they own. They give up open space, physical safety, and the best schools. Why do they choose to live there? Not because they like being crowded. Not because they like to live in dangerous, decaying neighborhoods. Most of them will say they are there simply because they think God can use them there.

Another possibility is to leave America completely. Yes, there are hungry people in America. Yes, there are people here who have never really understood what Jesus is about or who he is. But there are many more overseas, and in most countries, far fewer Christians. Ninety percent of the full-time Christian pastors and workers live in America, serving six percent of the world's people. So, through choosing careers that take them overseas, or through mission boards that work with national churches, thousands of Christians have chosen to leave the comfort of their own country. Some "suffer" more than others. But there is a cost for all. Why do they do it? Most of them would say it's because they think God wants them to.

Ninety percent of the full-time Christian pastors and workers live in America, serving six percent of the world's people.

Not everyone should go. God doesn't want all his people living in the inner city. He doesn't want all his people to leave America. But have you asked what he wants *you* to do?

Your Time

It's the most precious thing you own. How you spend it gives a pretty good reading on what you think is important. If you go running for an hour each day, it's safe to bet you consider running important.

What does God have to say about how you use your time?

Many Christians think the best thing they ever discovered was spending regular, disciplined time reading the Bible and praying.

They set aside a certain amount of time every day . . . ten minutes, a half hour, an hour . . . and devote it to God. No one I know who does this claims that it is a constant joy. Sometimes it takes sacrifice to find time. Often it is dull. But they still do it, because they think it's what God wants them to do with their time.

There are as many ways to spend time as there are Christians. Some give time to their grandparents, some to people in rest homes. Some spend time with non-Christians talking about God. Some do the administrative work that makes churches and Christian organizations roll. Some study textbooks so that they'll be able to become lawyers, ministers, writers.

Almost any use of time might be the way God wants you to go. But do you use your time only to please yourself? Or do you make the costly choice of finding out what God wants *you* to do with it?

Your Money

Jesus told his followers to sell their possessions and give the money to the poor. You don't have to believe that those words apply to everyone — though some do. But they must apply to someone.

So some Christians do without. Even if they make a lot of money, they give it away to people who need it more. They consciously choose to live at a simpler level . . . to eat less expensively . . . to drive older cars, or make do with public transportation . . . to live in uncomfortably small homes or apartments. They cite two reasons: first, by living poor, they find they have a better understanding of poor people . . . as well as a better understanding that their own lives depend on God, not on cash flow. Second, they feel that the money they don't use can help people who need it more — that the money that might buy a Saturday-night pizza would be better used by a family that worries every day whether there'll be even one meal. They feel that the food and resources they don't consume can be spread farther around the globe.

Even if God doesn't call you to live poor, that doesn't mean you're to live at the American Standard: "as well as possible." Just because you make money (or have it given to you) doesn't mean you have to spend it on yourself.

What does God want you to do with *your* money?

Your Dreams

Sometimes God wants you to give up your dreams. His dreams for you are better ones . . . but they may not seem attractive now.

Most of us dream of being married. Those dreams are usually fulfilled — we get married. But not everyone does, and not everyone should. The Bible calls singleness a gift. Are you willing to let God change your dreams?

Most of us dream of being popular . . . of being admired by the people who count. But Jesus wasn't terribly popular. Neither were his followers. They didn't set out to be unpopular, but their lives were different enough so they never fit in. And today, to be a Christian might mean leaving behind the style that spells popularity. Are you willing to let God change your dreams?

Most of us dream of being successful . . . of money and prestige. But if God wants you in a particular job . . . if he wants you working for a church, or in a low prestige job . . . then you will probably kiss "success" goodby. Are you willing to let God change *your* dreams?

I'm Only One Person

Young people are accused of being apathetic nowadays. Since students aren't marching for civil rights anymore, like they did in the '60s, people think we don't care. I don't think it's because we don't care, or because we can't think of anything to do. I think we sit back and do nothing because we *think* we're not important, and nothing we do really matters.

At the end of my first year of college, I volunteered for what I figured would be a neat vacation — a trip to Haiti with a bunch of other kids. The trip was a tour of various mission outposts on the island. We traveled through rustic cities and overgrown tropical forests visiting missionaries on their own turf, seeing them in their day-to-day work. We hadn't seen very much before a strange transformation in our group took place — we lost our "tourist" mentality and began aching for the people we saw.

For the first time, some of us came face-to-face with the worst of poverty, disease, and starvation. We saw the hollow look of despair and hopelessness in the eyes of too many helpless people; we knew that something had to be done. But what? We were only kids barely out of high school — what could we do?

Back at home, secure in our comfortable world, it would have been easy to get swallowed up again in books, classes, tests, and schedules. As the last of summer sped away, though, we tried to think of something we could do to make a difference. True, we didn't have the backing of NATO or some big world relief commission. We didn't know any senators or ambassadors. We had no money ourselves to send. What we did have was a small mountain of slides and snapshots we had taken on the trip. That was it — we would simply tell other people about what we had seen, show them through our slides what needed to be done and leave the rest to them.

Within a couple of months we were traveling throughout the state, singly or in groups, giving our slide shows. Different congregations gave donations and honorariums to help our "Haiti Fund" as we called it. Together we raised enough money to stock an entire mission hospital with much needed medicine and supplies, with enough left over to build a dining hall at a mission school. That was something I never would have dreamed could happen. We weren't the Red Cross, but we had made a difference.

Some people think that's foolish idealism. They say, "I'm only one person, what can I do? I don't matter at all." Well, I used to think that, until I found out one person *could* make a big difference. And Christians have an additional edge because God gives every Christian the power to accomplish his purpose. Together with other Christians I am part of a very powerful force: a force that can change the world.

by STEVE LAWHEAD

Love: Present And Future Tense

Bob Combs

Belonging to God's family means reaching out to others — in as many different ways as human needs come in. Christians are primarily "available" people; ready and willing to step into any situation that requires God's presence and understanding. Simply, we are to do what Jesus would do if he were here.

Without God	Someone stares at you across an empty room. Is he sizing you up? Is he laughing at you behind his stoic mask? You'll show him — you're better than he is. Unintimidated. Smarter. Throw him a haughty glance and walk away.
With God	The blank stare of a lonely stranger is an invitation to bridge the gap to another human being. The passive mask may hide deep feelings — a need to have someone to notice, to share. You take it on yourself to start a conversation. You make the first move. The rest is easy.
Without God	A church is a public building like the post office, or the YMCA. It's like a club, too. Many people crowd in on Sunday morning and the rest of the time it sits empty like a mausoleum. You drive by on Sunday mornings and you hear organ music and singing — it's so corny it's embarrassing. Don't those people know how silly they are?
With God	Each church building becomes a symbol for an unrealized dream: the house of God. Someday we'll live with him and that will be church enough for everyone, forever. Until then we gather in buildings large and small with other Christians to share a dream about the wonderful time to come — when the church will have no walls.
Without God	Why do they let those guys peddle that stuff in public? What a bother. Don't talk to them. Don't even look at them. Just walk by quickly and mumble, "No thanks. Not today." Not ever! They make you feel uncomfortable. They are throwbacks to another day — long past. Out of step with the times. Why don't they just let it die?
With God	Handing out tracts on the street corner takes a special kind of courage. You take the scolding looks, the hostile brush-offs. But just talking quietly with a friend about your beliefs takes courage, too. Maybe more. You care what your friend thinks of you, what he thinks of your faith. That can't be ignored. And at the risk of losing a friend, you're asked to share the secret of the universe. Such an important task — God would entrust it only to one of his children.

Philip Yancey

Without God

It's dog-eat-dog in this world. Nobody gets a free ride. It's too bad that some people have to suffer, but there are agencies to help those who need help. In fact, if people are too old or too helpless or uncaring to help themselves, let them call the Red Cross. They take care of that sort of thing, don't they?

With God

Love can be expressed to another person only through action. The love we are to show to others as Christians is a *demonstrated* love; it is meaningless without action, without observable results in the real world. Christian love restlessly seeks out tasks that only it can see, transforming ordinary workaday chores into acts of love.